If It Were Done

If It Were Done

Macbeth

and Tragic Action

James L. Calderwood

The University of Massachusetts Press

Amherst, 1986

Copyright © 1986 by
The University of Massachusetts Press
All rights reserved
Printed in the United States of America
Set in Linoterm Bembo at
The University of Massachusetts Press
Printed by Cushing-Malloy, Inc.
and bound by John Dekker & Sons

Library of Congress
Cataloging-in-Publication Data

Calderwood, James L.
    If it were done.

    Bibliography: p.
    Includes index.
    1. Shakespeare, William, 1564–1616. Macbeth.
I. Title.
PR2823.C28   1986   822.3'3   86–1264
ISBN 0–87023–534–6 (alk. paper)

For Robert B. Heilman, who taught me how to name the bigger light, and how the less

Contents

Preface

SHAKESPEARE'S PLAYS are like Wallace Stevens's blackbird; not even thirteen ways of looking at them will exhaust their capacity to appear. In what follows I am less ambitious than Stevens, essaying only three ways of looking at *Macbeth,* and even these are not sufficiently discrete to give us three different *Macbeth*s. Which is a negative way of saying that there are some likenesses among the ways of looking and some consistency in what is seen. In the first chapter I examine *Macbeth* from the perspective of *Hamlet,* on the assumption that if intertextuality has a bearing on Shakespeare's writing of *Macbeth,* then the most influential texts are likely to be his own prior plays. Thus I argue that *Macbeth* is as much indebted to *Hamlet* as it is to Holinshed's *Chronicles*—not of course for its historical content but for its modes and structures of presentation, and not because these are similar in the two plays but because they are almost systematically opposed, so that *Macbeth* emerges as a kind of "counter-*Hamlet*."

The second chapter focuses on what seems to me Shakespeare's major preoccupation in the play, the nature of tragic action. Just as in *Hamlet* he foregrounds theatricality as such, preventing us from blithely seeing through Burbage to Hamlet or through the Globe to Elsinore, so in *Macbeth* he foregrounds action so that it becomes not only a means of representation, a way of ordering the doings of the hero, but an object of representation. And insofar as action is the essence of tragedy, the play may be said to be a tragedy about the nature of tragedy. Not that the interest of *Macbeth* lies in its generic inheritance from the *Poetics* or other theories about the tragic. If Aristotle is relevant to *Macbeth*, it is in the same way that *Hamlet* is relevant, as a source of unlikeness. For action in *Macbeth* seems almost relentlessly to subvert the Aristotelean principles of wholeness, completeness, and limited magnitude, even of beginning, middle, and end. Perhaps needless to say, there is also a metadramatic aspect to this, and I make some effort to discern the ways in which Macbeth's dark deeds reflect Shakespeare's theatrical deed and to explore the effects of this on the audience. However, these matters are not worried at such length or with such an air of discovery that the book deserves a subtitle with the word "metadrama" in it, despite the vast increase in sales that would result.

Such a subtitle, for instance, would have little bearing on the third and longest chapter of the book, a sort of psycho-sociological study of violence and culture that is quite bereft of metadramatic visions and suchlike matters proceeding from the heat-oppressed brain. Instead I attempt to show how Shakespeare's undoing of deeds—his dismantling of the structure of action—extends itself into the fields of political and social order. Violence proves to be a barbarous dissolvent of the conventional differences by which Scots culture defines itself, eroding the borders between civilized society and savage nature, order and disorder, and even good and evil. At the same time violence is a sacred source of the very differences it destroys.

Since violence is a form of power, and power has recently acquired in some quarters the status of a transcendental signified, perhaps I should briefly mention some of the theoretical implications behind my view of *Macbeth*. The New Critical isolation of the text from history is now undergoing revision by a kind of New Historicism which draws fairly eclectically on Derrida, Lacan, Foucault, and Marxism to construe literature as an agency of political power.[1] I say "literature," although in keeping with the Derridean notion of *écriture* and Foucault's "discourse," many critics make no distinction between literature and what used to be thought of as non-literary or discursive texts.[2] Elevating discourse to the level of literature, nominally at least, may be useful insofar as it emphasizes the intertextual conversation wherein, say, this novel is a reply to prior romances or this anti-novel is a refutation of prior novels. Or, in the other direction, the non-distinction may be useful because it exposes the fictive aspects of historical, theological, and philosophical texts—or for that matter military field manuals—and thereby renders them vulnerable to the kind of close critical analysis formerly reserved for literature. In fact, however, very little of this kind of work is being done. Instead, dissolving the distinction between (Kantian) "disinterested" literature and "interested" discourse has enabled critics of power to uncover what Frederick Jameson calls the political unconscious in literature and in literary criticism as well. Thus many critics say that literature is always political, whatever its object of representation, because it contains a subtext of ideology—which usually means that it reflects the biases of a Western male-chauvinistic capitalist culture.[3]

Perhaps I should make it clear, then, that in my final chapter I am talking about manifestations of violence and power in Shakespeare's Scotland, not in King James's England. That is not because I think *Macbeth* or any other Shakespearean play is isolated from its social context, or because I think a political interpretation of it invalid, but only because this book does not address itself to such matters, as *Macbeth* does not address itself to the colonization of the New World.[4] A good deal has already been written about the possible influence on *Macbeth* of James I's views of Divine Right and witchery and of his and the nation's fears after the Gunpowder Plot,[5] and I can imagine a political interpretation of the play in which it might be argued that Macbeth's evil is tied to the Witches in order to make witchcraft the scapegoat for the English audience's religious and political anxieties. For if Catholics, Puritans, and Anglicans can agree on nothing else, they can at least agree to hate witches and, more importantly, the Devil, tutor and feeder of their covenly riots. Thus political subversion and even regicide, which some of the audience might be inclined to endorse, are attached to religious subversion of a sort all can condemn. By such theatrical means Shakespeare, spokesman for monarchy, would help consolidate the power of King James. Such an interpretation, however, if it were tenable, is probably insufficiently covert to qualify as a discovery of Shakespeare's political unconscious. Moreover, I have no way of knowing what

Shakespeare's political unconscious had in mind, or out of mind, if this is what it were up to, because I don't know how to interpret the interpretation. If the anxieties of the audience are funneled into witchcraft and the Devil, as I've suggested, are they then inflamed, as Plato would argue, or purged, as Aristotle would claim?

As a matter of fact I do suggest that Shakespeare works a form of deconstruction on some of the dominant political values of his time—order, degree, kingship, nature. But I doubt that it is done because he harbors deep reservations about English monarchy and the concepts that undergird it. Nothing we know about him leads us to believe he had any difficulty getting his plays past the religious and political censorship of the Revels Office. What evidence there is suggests he had an abiding belief in monarchy, law and order, religious moderation, capitalistic self-betterment, social climbing, male superiority, parental domination, and so forth—all the conservative shibboleths. Still, these, we might argue, are the attitudes of the man from Stratford, not the London playwright at his desk with his mind in Athens or along the coasts of Bohemia. So absorbed, he may lend the demeaning aspects of Antony's Egyptian revels a charming tint, but that does not stop the paterfamilias from Stratford from altering his will abruptly in 1616 to punish his philandering son-in-law. By the same token, if the playwright makes Shylock or Henry V puzzlingly ambiguous to us, the reason is not, I suspect, that he set out to debunk the prevailing stereotypes of the Jew or the marvelous monarch, but rather that the act of fictionalizing their experience obliged him to do justice to the complexities of individual character from which stereotypes are abstracted in the first place.

Thus instead of claiming that Shakespeare's political unconscious is voicing counter-cultural sentiments in *Macbeth,* I would argue that his artistic conscience is subverting his own more orthodox convictions. Just as Falstaff's natural passion for praying is thwarted by his purse-taking vocation, and it is no sin for a man to labor in his vocation, so Shakespeare's poetic calling must in some degree compromise his quotidian values. For although the London poet is condemned to occupy the same skin as the man from Stratford, a goose-quill is a powerful instrument of liberation.[6] This is especially so if the goose-quill is employed in writing plays, because the very nature of theater compels the playwright to an imaginative engagement with characters, action, and language in the context of living experience. The lyric and epic modes, issuing immediately or ultimately from one voice, have a unity of expression built into them. But dramatic dialogue entails opposition and contest and an imaginative ventriloquism on the playwright's part. Not for nothing that drama is thought to originate in the fragmentation of the Greek chorus or that the *agon* is still fundamental to its form. By its nature, theater has a kind of dispersive contentiousness that militates against the prefix "uni," as in such words as universal, univocal, and even unity. If we add to this Shakespeare's constitutional inability to look at blackbirds from one angle only—his famous negative capability—then his subversion of moral and political universals in his plays will be seen to serve the interests not of revolution but of a kind of contextualism that requires moral judgments to issue from the closest of encounters with particular cases.

If there is a political subtext in *Macbeth,* then, it is one that argues against the kind of generalized oppositions on which politics normally thrives. Or we might say that Shakespeare is a quiet revolutionary, one who does not fulminate on behalf of specific causes but who, merely by being true to his art, works in the long-range interests of a greater humanity. For instance, if we consider the role of women in *Macbeth,* we might at first glance take Lady Macbeth's unsexing of herself, her willingness to dash her child's brains out, and her evil influence on her husband as evidence of Shakespeare's male chauvinism. On reflection, however, we might feel that this defeminization of the lady erodes the Renaissance stereotype of woman, bridges the gap between male and female, and implies that evil is essentially masculine. (By the same token the Witches—who "should be women," Banquo says, "And yet your beards forbid me to interpret / That you are"—seem evil in part because they are not purely feminine.) Combine this with the fact that the hard-hearted lady later exhibits a noctural vulnerability to conscience so great as to imply her death by suicide, and the result is an image of woman that eludes the stereotypical.[7]

Or, to pursue the issue, if Lady Macduff is the properly feminine antithesis to Lady Macbeth, then Shakespeare stands accused of depicting his ideal woman, at least in this play, as appealingly maternal but pathetically helpless—obliged to play straight-mother to her son's wit, and rendered totally dependent on her husband's masculine power. Thus on the one hand to be assertively feminine like Lady Macbeth is to be defeminized in the direction of a monstrous masculinity, but on the other to be passively feminine like Lady Macduff is to be destroyed by male violence. If we are concerned with political power as it is mediated through the play, we will wonder what this "damned if you do, damned if you don't" plight of woman implies. Does it testify to Shakespeare's phallocentric inability to imagine a viable femininity? Or, to the contrary, does it represent his sympathetic portrayal of the unhappy status of women in Renaissance culture? Or, quite apart from his personal feelings, is it a product of his aesthetic need for a pattern of opposition in the structure of his play? The difficulty of making an entirely satisfactory judgment, even in the simplified form in which I have summarized the matter, is an index of the depth to which Shakespeare has embedded these issues in the experiential texture of his play.

In this connection perhaps I should repeat a view I expressed in another book, namely that criticism, however ill defined its goals and fierce its divisions, is or should be a corporate enterprise. "Should be" because it sometimes seems a kind of king-of-the-mountain competition in which one critic after another comes into power, usually by Macbeth-like means, struts and frets his brief hour on the stage, and then, would it were so, is heard no more.[8] This Darwinian situation prevails most desperately among literary theorists, but it is not unknown among Shakespeareans, where Critic A is besieged by Critic B, who is assaulted by Critic C, after whom trails a veritable Birnam Wood of armed and ambitious rivals. No doubt this is inevitable. Still, in lightheaded moments usually between a second and a third martini, I like to think we are all mutually engaged in the project of activating meanings in Shakespearean plays—not positivistic meanings deposited by Shakespeare to our account like half-crowns in a textual vault, and not on the other hand a semantic blank check on which we can write whatever we like, but meanings proliferated and flexibly constrained by the text.

If criticism is a joint venture, it follows that each interpretation is incomplete—merely one part of a larger interpretive project that will itself never be completed—and should be judged as such. A psychoanalytic account of *Macbeth* should not receive bad marks because it fails to assess patterns of imagery in the play, its mythic archetypes, stage history, Marxist or feminist subtext, or even its metadramatic epiphanies, any more than Shakespeare himself should be marked down for writing *Macbeth* instead of the *Odyssey*. The principle of polysemy should apply to critical methods as well as to semantics, since the danger lies not in our adopting partial perspectives but in our refusing to acknowledge and in some cases even to realize that we are doing so.

This view might seem overly permissive to some, an invitation to interpretive anarchy as the pluralism of thirteen ways of looking at a blackbird multiplies toward infinity. But anarchy is less a genuine danger than a scarecrow term to insure that the literary fields remain as they are. It is not a danger simply because what we see is constrained by the nature both of blackbirds and of our own ways of seeing. For the blackbird will not encourage us to see it as the Taj Mahal, and our shared optical structures will not let me see a blackbird and you see a swarm of quarks or a snowstorm of neutrinos. By the same token, *Macbeth* will not permit us to regard it as a treatise on horticultural practices in Scotland—despite Lady Macbeth's counsel that Macbeth look like "the innocent flower, / But be the serpent under it"—or as a farcical comedy, despite the Porter. Since language is our collective possession, not my private property, the text itself imposes a certain honesty upon my dealings with it.[9] And, from the other direction, the interpretive practices we share as critics, various as they are, keep our criticism within certain bounds. Though it may well be said of some modern critics, as Ben Jonson said of a fellow writer, that they "writ no language," language itself and critical language to boot bind us within the same enterprise. Even critical theorists have far more in common than their oft-contested differences would suggest, and among Shakespeareans the likenesses are yet more pronounced.

On the other hand some would argue that this sense of community is precisely the trouble with criticism today. On this view we are locked not only within the prison-house of language but within the prison-house of critical language as well, unwittingly fostering attitudes that preserve an unacceptable status quo instead of manning the intellectual barricades. The irony valorized by New Criticism, the undecidability and semantic free-play of poststructuralism, and the reflexiveness of metadrama seduce us away from political realities and leave us standing in life's voting booth muttering like Hamlet "words, words, words," while the Military Wound Research Labs go about their bloody business, the defense budget mounts, and nuclear autumn moves toward nuclear winter.

To this one can only reply that by comparison to newspaper editorials and thirty-second spots on national TV, literary criticism is not an impressive vehicle either for endorsing or overthrowing national hegemonies. Congress and the Politburo attend more closely to intelligence reports and campaign contributions than to Marxist or feminist or bourgeois readings of Shakespeare. Yet because that is so at a time when six million Africans are starving and the major powers seem bent on converting the earth to charcoal, as critics we may well feel that, Falstaff to the contrary, it *is* a sin for a man to labor in his vocation. Still, if the prospect of nuclear winter trivializes Shakespearean criticism, what does it not trivialize? Treat every man after his desert in this respect and no one should 'scape whipping. Fortunately, however, a vocation need not stop one's ears to other callings. Since we are all independent persons as well as critics we are free to write, send checks, or march in behalf of whatever causes we choose.[10]

Let me, however, make my way out of these thickets of polemical theory, somewhat like Antigonus in *The Winter's Tale*—"Exeunt, pursued by a bear"—by noting that in addition to the formal chapters that follow I have appended a few supplements. It seems appropriate that the end of a book about a play whose actions have no end should itself resist a rounded closure by trailing a few threads of its argument behind. These constitute, in computerese, a kind of random access memory—a wayward pack of clarifications and confusions that for one reason or another could not find lodging in the main text, yet that seemed sufficiently relevant to deserve some sort of belated say in the matter. In other words they are the best part of the book—or at least the briefest, which probably comes to the same thing.

Finally, since my theme here has been critical community, let me take time to acknowledge some of my own creditors in that department. My oldest debt, to a brilliant critic and teacher, as well as a fine friend, is registered in the dedication. More recently, I am grateful to Norman Rabkin for reading portions of the manuscript with his characteristic generosity and perceptiveness; to Kirby Farrell for various kindnesses in the beaten way of friendship; to Richard Abrams and John Blanpied for unusually swift, conscientious, and helpful readings of the text; and to Bruce Wilcox for ushering the manuscript through the editorial mills of the Press with marvelous expedition and engaging grace. Arthur Kinney has kindly allowed me to include material that first appeared in *English Literary Renaissance,* 14, no. 1 (1984), and J. Leeds Barroll and Barry Gaines have allowed me to include an expanded version of an article that first appeared in *Shakespeare Studies,* 17 (1985). I should note also that the text I am using throughout is that of David Bevington in *The Complete Works of Shakespeare,* 3rd edition (Glenview, Ill.: Scott, Foresman, 1980).

If It Were Done

One

Macbeth: Counter-Hamlet

 HEN SHAKESPEARE came to write *Macbeth* I think he found himself guided somewhat obscurely by his awareness of what he had done, or rather not done, in *Hamlet*. Probably that's true of the writing of several of his subsequent plays. That is, one might profitably study, say, *Othello* or *Lear* not merely in their own right but as post-*Hamlet* plays, because the range and complexity of *Hamlet*'s language, styles, and forms make it a theatrical matrix for the plays that not merely follow it but also repeat it, vary it, suppress it, or take off from it. But I think *Macbeth* has a special relation to *Hamlet*. In some respects it is like a photographic negative of the earlier play, not merely different from it as the other tragedies are, but the inverse of it—a counter-*Hamlet*. That has a metaphysical ring to it, as though under pressure of the great mass of its language (not to mention the critical language with which it has been freighted), *Hamlet* collapsed into a literary black hole and emerged into a parallel uni-

verse of anti-matter as *Macbeth*. But this astrophysical notion goes awry for several instructive reasons. For one thing black holes emit no light, while *Hamlet,* judging from the perpetual squint of its critics, is still there blinding us all. For another, in addition to being invisible, anti-matter is supposed also to be identical to its ordinary counterpart, but no one would suggest that Shakespeare's two tragedies mirror one another. Finally, anti-matter is a negative energy state, whereas in the Shakespearean universe *Hamlet* is best characterized by negation and absence, where *Macbeth* is, I suggest, positively charged.

So if *Macbeth* is a counter-*Hamlet,* it is not in these ways. Let me abandon these ethereal anti-matters and come down to earth, or at least to a text. I want to examine *Macbeth* in light of certain concepts that play a prominent role in *Hamlet*—concepts like time, action, and mediation—in hopes of bringing to the fore some aspects of *Macbeth,* perhaps some of *Hamlet* too, that might otherwise pass unnoticed.[1] Most of these notions center in action, not language, because language seems to me less of an issue in the later play. Although eloquent in himself, Macbeth is not interested in language as Hamlet is. In fact, like Othello and Lear, he could profit from some of the Dane's verbal sophistication.[2] But despite what his wife says, he is most anxious "to catch the nearest way," and the nearest way is almost never a verbal way—which is why it is Hamlet's way. Macbeth's way is action. Let us begin there then.

ACTION

In both plays a central concern of the action is action itself—the act of revenge that remains unperformed for so long by Hamlet, the act of regicide that is performed so soon by Macbeth. The location of these acts has a significant bearing on the constitution of the two plays. Hamlet's revenge takes place at the end of the play, so that for about four "acts" the focus is not on action but on pre-action—on all that deters, calls in question, and at last prepares for action. On the other hand, Macbeth's murder of Duncan occurs relatively early in his play, so that the focus is on what Macbeth himself most fears, consequences—on all that lingers out and follows from an action. This stress on action is so great in

Macbeth as to merit special sustained attention—hence the following chapter, which examines the issue of doing and undoing in the play. Let me comment here only briefly on the origins of action.

In each play the instigation to act has a preternatural source. Hamlet receives ghostly instructions, Macbeth witchy predictions. However, the Ghost's instructions are in the active voice, the Witches' predictions in the passive. Hamlet is told what *to do*—take revenge, kill the King—Macbeth is merely told what is *to be*—his own kingship. When Macbeth converts this prediction of a future state of royal being into an active invitation to kill a king, he very nearly reverses the process by which Hamlet converts the Ghost's command to kill a king into a prolonged exploration of his own state of being as a disenfranchised prince.

As a minor point, we might observe that the swiftness with which each man acts is "predicted" by the way in which the preternatural invitations to act are dramatically presented. That is, the postponement of Hamlet's revenge throughout the play is in keeping with the postponement of his initial meeting with the Ghost. In Act I the Ghost does not come directly to Hamlet as it does in the Closet Scene, but arrives by stages, appearing twice to the soldiers and once again for the benefit of Horatio before confronting Hamlet himself. Who is the Ghost to complain later of Hamlet's roundaboutness?

By the same token, the swiftness with which Macbeth dispatches Duncan after meeting the Witches is in keeping with the abruptness with which they appear to him and Banquo on the heath: "What are these / So withered and so wild in their attire?" Of course the Witches' meeting with Macbeth is also deferred—they appear in the opening scene of the play to announce that they will meet with Macbeth later, "when the hurlyburly's done." But this is only a momentary postponement, not as with the Ghost an ostentatiously prolonged process that makes us conscious of impediments and intermediaries.

INBETWEENNESS AND IMAGINATION

To speak of impediments and intermediaries is to raise the issue of inbetweenness, which constitutes a significant difference between the modes of the two plays. In *Hamlet* the middle—the interim, the gap, the space between two persons or events—is always clogged. Direct action and immediate presence are hard to come by. Claudius cannot deal directly with Hamlet but only through such sifting agents as Polonius, Rosencrantz and Guildenstern, Ophelia, Gertrude, and finally Laertes. In the duel of mighty opposites these are the royal weapons, whose thrusts Hamlet parries with a targe of assumed madness embossed with puns and riddling figures. Only when these intermediaries have been swept aside by death—and when Hamlet's madplay and wordplay have been abandoned in the Graveyard Scene—is the space between the King and the Prince cleared for a mortal engagement. Thus one movement of the play is through an obstructive mediateness toward immediacy, in accord with Polonius's principle of finding directions out by means of indirections.

If *Hamlet* demonstrates the resistant force of inbetweenness, *Macbeth* features an increasingly easy erasure of inbetweenness in the interests of immediacy. Consider for instance the gap between the word and the thing. In *Hamlet* this is the gap between the Ghost's command to revenge and Hamlet's final act of revenge, a gap that is writ wide by Hamlet's infamous delay. In *Macbeth,* on the other hand, the gap is between the Witches' prophecies and Macbeth's future kingship, a gap that would have been much wider than it is had Macbeth not erased it by regicide. Killing Duncan kills the interim.

But even before the actual murder Macbeth erases the interim between prophecy and kingship when on the heath he has "horrible imaginings" of the murder of Duncan. Of course Hamlet is given to imagining also, but according to his own analysis "thinking too precisely on the event" deters rather than promotes action. And though he constantly berates himself for it, he clearly prefers the capaciousness of the imagination, where everything is possible, to the confinements of action, where one must do one thing and not another, let alone all others. For Hamlet an imagined revenge in the unspecified future—

> when [Claudius] is drunk asleep, or in his rage,
> Or in the incestuous pleasure of his bed,

> At game a-swearing, or about some act
> That has no relish of salvation in it

—takes precedence over a revenge that is as immediate as the blade in his hand (3.3). For Macbeth on the other hand a murder that "yet is but fantastical" may momentarily smother function in surmise, but surmise is not the thing itself, and he is anxious to pass from illusion to reality.

For Hamlet imagination is an impediment to action, even at times an end in itself, whereas for Macbeth it is the genesis and agency of action. Duncan's murder takes place in the mind before it occurs in the castle, and the route from the subjunctive "If it were done" to the indicative "I go, and it is done" is paved by murderous fancies. This is most compactly demonstrated in Act 2, Scene 1, when a "dagger of the mind" creates a dagger in the hand, and an imagined half-world of darkness prowled by wolves and withered murder provides a scene in which Duncan's death is a foregone conclusion.

Actually Macbeth's imagination is something of a paradox, since it is both a get-between and a go-between for action. As a get-between it occupies the space between the desire to act and the act itself, and hence can even deter action, as in the Hamlet-like "If it were done" soliloquy. At that point Macbeth is momentarily deterred from acting by considerations of justice, duty, and emotion, all arguing that he should get between Duncan and his murderer, "not bear the knife [himself]." On the other hand, as a go-between Macbeth's imagination envisages and conduces to action, most obviously in the "Is this a dagger that I see" soliloquy. As his murderous career advances, however, his imagination becomes less and less a get-between. The retarding mediations of the mind yield to forwarding intermediaries outside—the three murderers of Banquo, and those who slaughter Macduff's family. Yet even in these later instances Macbeth is still taking the most direct and murderous route to the satisfaction of his desires. It is not so much that he has relinquished action to others as that he has extended his range of evildoing. We simply have Macbeth taking action at a distance.

This impression is created largely by Macbeth's remarks about erasing inbetweenness within himself. The moral imagination that momentarily deters him from killing Duncan and that unmans him in the presence of Banquo's ghost must be totally elided. It is a matter between the heart or head that conceives a villainy and the hand that enacts it: "Strange things I have in head, that will to hand, / Which must be acted ere they may be scanned" (3.4.140). And after seeing the Witches and then hearing of the flight of Macduff, he says

> From this moment
> The very firstlings of my heart shall be
> The firstlings of my hand.   (4.1.146)

Having thus eliminated the middleman conscience, he orders the castle of Macduff seized and all within given to the sword. With Macduff safely abroad, Macbeth lashes out at anyone or anything that stands between him and his ambitions—a pointless but typically inhuman act by a dehumanized tyrant, a man who has ceased to be a man by virtue of having closed the gap of humankindness that properly exists between the heart and the hand. Thus when Macduff learns of his woes in far-off England, Macbeth seems almost physically present, in part because of Malcolm's imitation of him when he tests Macduff (4.3.1–114), and in part because of the contrast between the saintly hand of Edward the Confessor, whose royal touch cures "evil" so easily, and the diabolic hand of Macbeth that reaches forth its evil in this scene and touches Macduff. Macbeth has not merely erased inbetweenness; he has extended himself everywhere.

REACTIVE/INITIATIVE

If we transpose inbetweenness from space to time we could think of it as the present, the point of transition between past and future. From this perspective the present of *Hamlet* is reactive and retentive, that of *Macbeth* initiative and protentive. In this section let me look at the opposition of the reactive and the initiative, reserving the retentive and protentive for later.

Both heroes, as we have seen, react to preternatural instigations to action; but whereas Hamlet continues in a reactive vein throughout the play, having let the initiative pass to Claudius, Macbeth is himself a source of action. There is a certain appropriateness in Hamlet's being reactive, because revenge itself is reactive and past-conscious. Though often self-perpetuating, as in feuds, its ideal aim is a point for point matching or even overmatching of "re-venge" to "venge" so that the latter is symbolically cancelled. As René Girard has emphasized, violence fosters mimesis.[3] If Hamlet's father was taken full of bread, so must Claudius be; and if Claudius incestuously pursued a union with Gertrude in life, then so metaphorically must he in death: "Drink off this potion. Is thy union here? Follow my mother." The present takes cues from the past in hopes of evening things up and so making an end. The essential reactiveness of revenge is underscored in *Hamlet* by having it issue from a fencing match, where thrust is normally answered by riposte, as the thrust of the King's plot is answered by Hamlet's quick retaliation.

To some extent Macbeth, like Hamlet, reacts to supernatural soliciting. "Soliciting," however, is Macbeth's word (1.3.130). The Witches solicit no one; they merely reveal the future. Macbeth's imagination invents the murder of Duncan. The heinousness of the act is owing in part to its being unprovoked and unprecedented. Perhaps a kind of precedent consists in the recently defeated rebels, who also sought Duncan's life and crown. But slaughter in the open field is one thing and murder in private chambers another; and Macbeth, who engages in both, registers the difference between the two as he passes full of self-loathing from field to chamber to do a deed so grotesquely original that it cannot be named. By the conventions of his assignment, Hamlet, like all revengers, is required to model himself upon his enemy. Had he done so more readily, he had made an end. Had Macbeth modeled himself upon Duncan, he had never made a beginning. But he does. His is not a reactive but an initiative mode. He makes a radical break with what was and sets out ambitiously for what is to be.

The distinction between reactive and initiative may even apply to the composition of the two plays. *Hamlet* is of course patterned on the lost revenge play known as the *Ur-Hamlet,* presumably written by Thomas Kyd. Thus a Shakespeare who takes revenge-play instruction from Kyd's old-*Hamlet* is like his hero taking orders for revenge from Old Hamlet his father. Each is given the paternal command, "Remember me!" Because Shakespeare's re-write and Hamlet's revenge are both modeled on a prior act, the problem arises how to maintain a certain likeness to the model without sacrificing the unlikeness that makes for individuality. Such a problem does not present itself in *Macbeth,* however, because Shakespeare's models for this play are not dramatic but narrative: Holinshed's *Chronicles* and perhaps Page's translation of Buchanan's *Rerum Scoticarum Historia.* Individuality and differ-ence are almost guaranteed when the narrative mode is transposed into the dramatic. Hero and playwright are both engaged in a deed without precedent—Macbeth's murder of a king and Shake-speare's dramatization of Macbeth's murder of a king.[4]

PAST/FUTURE

If Danish history was of little interest to Shakespeare when he wrote *Hamlet,* its fictive past is an almost obsessive concern of his hero. For the grieving Prince the past, or his illusion of the past, is a repository of all that is good and grand—a noble and royal father, a loving mother, the beauteous and innocent Ophelia, loyal schoolfellows, and himself the heir-apparent glass of fashion and mold of form. When that world of dignity and grace is ex-posed by the Ghost's tale as merely the bright surface of corrup-tion, Hamlet is asked not so much to premeditate revenge as to remember, the last words of that ghostly tale being "Remember me!" And in a sense Hamlet makes his own way through the play much as Ophelia says he left her chamber, "with his head over his shoulder turned," yearning backwards as though where he has been were infinitely preferable to where he must go. To supple-ment his own remembering, he takes it upon himself to summon up remembrance of things past in others as well. His production of "The Mousetrap" calls up guilty memories, if not true peni-tence, in the normally forward-looking Claudius; and even the oblivious Gertrude can be made to remember how easily she forgets if she is forced to examine the "counterfeit presentiment of two brothers" and to suffer the pangs of her son's daggerlike speech. Wielded verbally on Ophelia and bloodily on her father, Hamlet's daggers produce a distract maid whose own mad words sound a flowery keynote to the play:

> There's rosemary, that's for remembrance; pray you, love, remember.
> And there is pansies, that's for thoughts.

"A document in madness," her brother cries, "thoughts and remembrance fitted" (4.5.177). A document in revenge also, could Hamlet but fit the two to action. But when the revenge comes it is not by an intention based on retention, a plot to revenge ("thoughts and remembrance fitted"), but in rash reaction to the plots of others. Finally, even when the revenge is done and the hero under strictest arrest, his dying concerns remain retrospective as he commandeers Horatio's voice to "report [him] and [his] cause aright / To the unsatisfied."

Macbeth on the other hand is prophetic and premeditative. In contrast to the elaborate preparations in *Hamlet* for the Ghost's tale about past evils, the opening scene with the Witches is not designed to call up the past—there is scarcely any exposition early in the play—but to forecast a meeting with Macbeth on the heath. That later meeting introduces the prophecies that cast the hero's thoughts and the audience's expectations even further into the future. Then a series of anticipatory imaginings and conversations between Macbeth and his wife lead step by step to the murder of Duncan. Once Duncan is in his grave the murder of Banquo is forecast by Macbeth's meeting with the two murderers, and finally the ending of the play is portended by the apparitions and the Witches' second set of prophecies, which assure the uneasy tyrant that he is safe unless the impossible occurs and which assure the audience that the impossible will indeed occur.[5]

To these outside prophecies and forecasts correspond Macbeth's inner readyings for the future. Like his wife, he can close the temporal gap between "is" and "will be" and "feel now / The future in the instant" (1.5.57). Although he wants something more substantial than an imagined future, imagining is his means of acquiring it. Not merely does he premeditate his acts but he imagines scenes in which they can properly take place:

> Now o'er the one half-world
> Nature seems dead, and wicked dreams abuse
> The curtained sleep; witchcraft celebrates
> Pale Hecate's offerings, and withered murder,
> Alarumed by his sentinel, the wolf,
> Whose howl's his watch, thus with his stealthy pace
> With Tarquin's ravishing strides, towards his design
> Moves like a ghost.   (2.1.50)

> Light thickens, and the crow
> Makes wing to the rooky wood;
> Good things of day begin to droop and drowse,
> Whiles night's black agents to their preys do rouse.
>
>   (3.2.53)

Thus whereas in *Hamlet* future action is repeatedly deferred and frustrated, in *Macbeth* it is constantly anticipated and impending. The play is full of imagined scenes of darkness and evil receptively awaiting the murderous acts that will occur within them.

If Hamlet edges reluctantly into the future, leaving an ideal world behind him, Macbeth rushes with increasing speed toward an ideal future that keeps receding before him. Macbeth forgoes one good for a greater good in prospect. Yet that greater good— his possession of present crown and future succession—is no more attainable than the means by which he seeks it are erasable. A Tantalus figure in time, Macbeth cannot quite reach the desired future because he cannot extricate himself from the past. On the heath his "horrible imaginings" collapse tomorrow into today as he feels "the future in the instant," but when he contemplates Duncan's murder in his "If it were done" soliloquy it is the completedness of the doing that he desires, the swift conversion of a future "to do" into a past "done" without the intermediate discomforts of a present doing.

But that is precisely what does not happen. The act that, once performed, should be altogether done and sealed securely in the

past remains instead disastrously undone and still to do. The following chapter will expand upon this point, but for the moment
let me observe merely that each of Macbeth's murderous deeds
remains incomplete. The present will not conveniently recede
into a closed past. Ultimately the unresolved past reenters the
present in the form of the army of Malcolm and Macduff and
takes possession of the future, even as the escaped Fleance will
take possession of the long-range future by means of James I and
the Stuart succession. In pursuit of the future, Macbeth has imagined murders before their time, become king before his time,
made Duncan, Banquo, and Macduff's family die before their
time. And now time takes its revenge on Macbeth. At the end it is
appropriate that he to whom the future has been so infinitely
desirable, the locus of all meaning, should register his losses by
a total indifference to it. His once passionate hope that the future
might enter and become the present—that the prophetic "hereafter" of "All hail, Macbeth, that shall be king hereafter" might
be "here"—is fulfilled in the death of his wife, who "should have
died hereafter" but did so now, before her time. In Macbeth's
famous speech that follows he acknowledges the unalterable se-
quentiality of time, the metronomic "tomorrow and tomorrow
and tomorrow" of the future as it keeps coming in at its own
pace. Yet it comes mockingly at his pace too. For these trivial
tomorrows are also "today," becoming "now" by virtue of
Macbeth's use of the present tense—"creeps in," not "will creep
in"—and they bring with them only death and a sense of pervasive meaninglessness.

INTERIOR/EXTERIOR

Having glanced at the ways in which Shakespeare temporalizes
action, let us see how he spatializes it with reference to such concepts as interior and exterior. Somewhat roundaboutly, let me
begin by associating these notions with sleep and wakefulness. In
his most famous soliloquy Hamlet says that to sleep forever is
a "consummation devoutly to be wished" were it not at the risk of
bad dreams. "Consummation" is apt here, since it is poised between the meanings of fulfillment and extinction, much as sleep is

poised between life and death. In keeping with the death-plus or life-minus character of sleep, Hamlet's father passes not directly from life to death as Old Fortinbras did in the field but, aided by an application of hebenon, from a midday sleep in his orchard to death. Looking like death, sleep may readily become it. But it may also be a shelter from life's slings and arrows, as it is in Hamlet's case.

If sleep is construed as a deathlike shutting of the eyes to life's affairs, a kind of faint that obliterates oppression, then it can be seen to symbolize inaction in a play that calls insistently for one revengeful act. Thus Hamlet compares himself unfavorably to the militant Fortinbras by saying

> How stand I then,
> That have a father killed, a mother stained,
> Excitements of my reason and my blood,
> And let all sleep?   (4.4.56)

Peaking like "John-a-dreams" (2.2.567), he metaphorically lets his revenge sleep throughout the middle of the play, as the figure of Revenge literally sleeps throughout the middle of Kyd's *Revenger's Tragedy.* That is, the intense subjectivity of Hamlet's soliloquies and his psychological isolation from the court world during this period of delay can be likened to sleep and dream.[6] The dreams he has are all bad dreams; otherwise he could be content though bounded in a nutshell. And having suffered life's bad dreams, in which his uncle kills his father and marries his mother, he fears all dreams, even those that might disturb the sleep of death (3.1.67). If his revenge is to awake, however, he must himself stir from inward dreams and take his place in the outward world where kings are killed. But he cannot do so until he has slept very near to death itself. Thus in the last act, when he describes to Horatio the decisive actions he took at sea, wakefulness saves his life and releases him from Denmark's prison:

> Sir, in my heart there was a kind of fighting
> That would not let me sleep. Methought I lay
> Worse than the mutines in the bilboes.   (5.2)

This half-sleep from which he wakes is in some symbolic degree the half-sleep of his delayed revenge, and the swift actions that follow—his rewriting of the King's deadly commission and his felicitous boarding of the pirate ship—suggest that he has become fully alert to the dangers of the world and to the need to counter them forcefully, even brutally. From sleep and dream Hamlet emerges, as he defines it, into a state of wakeful "readiness" that seems prerequisite to his revenge.

In *Hamlet,* then, sleep and dream are associated with the hero's dilatory subjectivity, in which all outward matters are interiorized as soliloquy and wordplay, and from which he must waken to the exigencies of action if he and his play are ever to make an end. In *Macbeth* on the other hand subjectivity is not so much opposed to action as in league with it. On the heath, "rapt" by supernatural solicitings, Macbeth can observe that "function / Is smothered in surmise," and yet the "horrible imaginings" that momentarily numb him to his surroundings nevertheless contain the murder of Duncan *in potentia,* a waking nightmare that will become real. Still there is a point where the borders between fantasy and fact, potency and action, dissolve, and we are not sure if the murder has fully made its exit from Macbeth's imagination. Thus in Act 2, Scene 1, Macbeth is ostensibly preparing to depart for bed when the hallucinated dagger appears, marshalling into existence a real dagger a moment later. Then Macbeth imagines a dead world in which "wicked dreams abuse / The curtained sleep" and sets out somnambulistically toward the sleeping Duncan. Afterwards, outside the chambers, he is like a man abruptly awakened from a murderous nightmare, unsure whether he has only dreamed or actually done the deed. He keeps remembering a voice that cried "Sleep no more! / Macbeth does murder sleep":

> Still it cried "Sleep no more!" to all the house;
> "Glamis hath murdered sleep, and therefore Cawdor
> Shall sleep no more; Macbeth shall sleep no more."

And from this point on Macbeth does go sleepless, lying "in restless ecstasy" and envying Duncan, who "after life's fitful fever . . . sleeps well" (3.2.24). Toward the end this sleeplessness takes its toll. Lady Macbeth sleepwalks her way to a guilty death, and

Macbeth, like a man kept awake so long that he can feel nothing ("I have almost forgot the taste of fears" [5.5.9]), dully regards it as merely a premature instance of the inevitable exit from life's fitful illusions.

PLAY/REALITY

One reason for Hamlet's notorious delay is that his act of revenge is defined like all acts by its scene of enactment, and the Danish scene is deeply contaminated. In a Denmark foully "tainted" the hero is charged by the Ghost both to act and in the process to "Taint not thy mind" (1.5.87). How Hamlet is to do this, to venture into a contaminated world and kill a king while remaining uncontaminated himself, he is not informed. Attempting to puzzle it out, he finds temporary recourse in transforming action into an "act"—into madplay, wordplay, and finally a stage play. This kind of acting, which occupies a space somewhere between inaction and action, is at least untainted by guilt. Players, after all, are the perfect criminals, capable night after night of robberies and murders for which they are never indicted.

But of course their victims never bring charges, having no evidence of injury. Hamlet's major act in this mode is his rewriting and staging of "The Murder of Gonzago," the performance of which frights the King with false fire but, alas, draws no blood. It is evident that if Hamlet is to perform his ghostly assignment he must graduate from acting to action, from madman to revenger. And so he does. In fact when the revenge takes place it illustrates this process graphically, issuing as it does from an inner-"play," the swordplay of Hamlet and Laertes. But let me bate that point for a moment.

Hamlet uses madplay, wordplay, and even stageplay as substitutes for revengeful action, though each is sharply edged and draws some inward blood from his enemies and friends alike. In *Macbeth* there are comparatively few references to play and small stress on theatricality. But let me sketch what there is. The first major reference is Macbeth's line upon learning that he is thane now of both Glamis and Cawdor:

> Two truths are told
> As happy prologues to the swelling act
> Of the imperial theme.   (1.3.127)

One effect of this is to lend an air of inevitability to the notion of drama by associating the Witches' prophecies with an already-written play scheduled for performance on the stage of Scotland. Phrasing it in this manner, Macbeth attempts to preserve a certain innocence for himself. He who "wouldst not play false, / And yet wouldst wrongly win" (1.5.21), as his wife says, cannot be accused of playing false if he is merely acting his part in this large drama of the times.

In keeping with this, Macbeth can murder Duncan only by writing and acting in his own "play." Thus in the hallucinated dagger scene we see him transforming himself from an honored subject and host about to retire to bed into an extreme version of the stage villain—"withered murder" striding like Tarquin toward his design—about to do an evil deed upon a stage whose imaginative setting he describes to the audience like a prologue:

> Now o'er the one half-world
> Nature seems dead, and wicked dreams abuse
> The curtained sleep; witchcraft celebrates
> Pale Hecate's offerings . . .   (2.1.50)

Given such a scene an act of horror is not only fitting but virtually inevitable.[7] Thus in Duncan's bedchamber Macbeth's "act" becomes a regicidal deed. Unlike "The Murder of Gonzago," "The Murder of King Duncan" draws real blood, enough to incarnadine the seas.

Afterwards, when Macbeth exits from the scene he is like an actor who only gradually distinguishes self from role and knows his deed is real: "I am afraid to think what I have done; / Look on it again I dare not." Nor dare he look upon himself: "To know my deed, 'twere best not know myself." Best too that others not know him. And so he adopts the role of affable if somewhat uncommunicative host leading Macduff to Duncan's door, then of stunned hearer of the murderous fact, and finally of vengeful sub-

ject unable to restrain "the expedition of [his] violent love" (2.3).
But despite his innocent roles the first fiction is indelible. Like
Antonio in *The Tempest,* who plays the ducal role of his brother
Prospero until in his mind he becomes the Duke (1.2.90 ff.),
Macbeth plays "withered murder" in Duncan's chambers and
then becomes what he played in all Scotland. But to his unusual
credit at some level of consciousness Macbeth the man—he who
"wouldst not play false"—knows Macbeth the actor for what he
villainously is, and rejects him. By then, however, it is far too
late. Life has become a "walking shadow," the transient performance of a "poor player." But this image of theater does not
entail a fictionality that erases guilt. Macbeth has bloodied all the
stages in Scotland, and will make no easy exit.

Let me return to the issue of play and action. In *Hamlet,* I suggested earlier, wordplay and madplay substitute for and hence
defer the revengeful act the hero is commanded to perform;
whereas in *Macbeth,* as we have just seen, role-playing enables the
hero to perform an act he cannot manage in his own person.
When Hamlet at last does kill Claudius, he seems to have passed
from play to reality. But that is not entirely the case, since in
Hamlet what is most real is, paradoxically, play itself, whereas the
reverse is true in *Macbeth.* Let me clarify this by comparing the
killing actions with which the two plays end.

The meeting of Macbeth and Macduff climaxes a demystifying
process in which the Witches' prophecies of apparently supernatural events—Birnam Wood moving to Dunsinane, a man not
born of woman—come true in quite ordinary ways. This strip-
ping of the supernatural to the natural—a moving wood to
camouflaged soldiers and an invulnerable Macbeth to mortality—
leaves us simply with two armies fighting for Scotland and then
with two leaders fighting for their lives. This stress on the natural
in Scotland runs parallel to the stress on the realistic in the Globe.
We have two levels of action—stage action and *Macbeth*-action—
and we are invited to see through the one to the other, to see for
instance not two actors swinging property-swords but Macbeth
and Macduff dueling to the death.

But consider the swording at the end of *Hamlet.* Again we have two levels of action, on-stage and in-court, and we are asked to transform actors with property-swords into Hamlet and Laertes fencing. "Fencing," however, not dueling to the death. For fencing converts dueling into play, into sword-"play," where the stakes are not one's life but Barbary horses on one side and French rapiers and poinards with their assigns on the other. This complicates everything—especially because in keeping with the principle of "to be and not to be" in *Hamlet,* the swordplay is both play (i.e., fencing on Hamlet's part) and not-play (i.e., murderous attack on Laertes' part). But then again it is not both play and not-play but all-play—pretense—since Hamlet as fencer is pretending to duel and Laertes as duelist is pretending to fence, though to judge from their actions they are both doing the same thing, whatever it is. Then, with the discovery of the unbated foil, both cease playing and are really dueling. With this quick passage from play to deadly dueling, the swordplay in this scene coalesces with the overall metaphoric duel throughout the play featuring the "mighty opposites" Hamlet and Claudius, between whose "fell incensed points" so many die (5.2.61). Now death as a scoreable "touch" on the surface of the body finds its way to more penetrable stuff when Hamlet cries "The point envenomed too? Then, venom, to thy work!"

From this perspective it seems that in *Hamlet* as in *Macbeth* play conducts the hero to reality; "acting" conduces to murderous action. However, the paradoxes of the sword-"play" cannot help alerting the audience to the stageplay in the Globe where two actors are playing two characters who are also playing in their different and confusing ways. Thus as dueling becomes a reality in Elsinore, play becomes a reality in the Globe—the outer play that encloses all inner-play. What seems real in *Hamlet* keeps turning into play by virtue of Shakespeare's metadramatic paradoxes, whereas what is stage-play in *Macbeth*—the hero's imaginings, the Witches' prophecies—turns into reality in Scotland. For all its Witches and demonism, *Macbeth* is a positive and ultimately realistic play, whereas *Hamlet* negates its realities again and again with a self-frustrating vengeance.

MEANING WITHOUT AND WITHIN

Action in *Hamlet* is figured as external to the hero, a realm he must gird himself to enter, but action in *Macbeth* originates within the hero and issues outward. Perhaps this is because in *Hamlet* the public world is poisoned, whereas in *Macbeth* the hero's imagination is contaminated. At any rate, having given a kind of spatial location to action, let us attempt something similar with meaning.

In a broad linear sense *Hamlet* moves "toward" and *Macbeth* "from" meaning. Thus Hamlet begins on a note of meaninglessness as he delivers a soliloquy about "how weary, stale, flat, and unprofitable" are all the uses of the world, at least to his dejected mind. Whatever illusions of value he still retains are destroyed by the Ghost's story, and as a result he spends much of the rest of the play measuring how far into evil and absurdity the world has fallen from what it should have been. Somewhat mysteriously, however, by indirections that take him first to sea and then through the graveyard, he arrives at a state of watchful acquiescence in which he has come to terms with death, defers to the shapings of divinity, and discerns a special providence in the fall of sparrows, not to mention those of Danish princes.

Macbeth's movement "from" meaning is less anfractuous. From a world of just-recovered order and significance in which he has bought "golden opinions from all sorts of people" (1.7.33), he passes by way of murder and tyranny to a point where his own meaningless acts are paralleled by his feeling that all of life is an idiot's tale signifying nothing.

Hamlet's plight is complicated by the fact that he inherits a world already contaminated by murder, incest, and royal lies in which he must somehow act without tainting his mind. Revenge in such circumstances would seem difficult enough. But Hamlet, being Hamlet, will arrange to make it more difficult still. Why settle for a relatively straightforward assignment like killing the King when he can transform it into a cosmic affair? Thus for him, "Kill the King" is readily translated into "The time is out of joint. O cursed spite, / That ever I was born to set it right" (1.5.189). As time's orthopedist in Elsinore, his business, he assumes, is not merely to excise from ailing Denmark its hidden imposthume the King but to diagnose all the symptoms of the pursy times—disease, degeneration, death. He will constitute an investigative committee of one to prescribe for Denmark, meanwhile tabling the motion to kill the King.

Death is Hamlet's most fixed obsession, beginning of course with the death of his father. Death is in abundance at the opening of *Macbeth* too, but it is battlefield death—rebellion in the open field, not a sly poisoning in the garden—and it attends the quelling of disorder, not its crowning. Thus for a brief period after the hurlyburly's done, order reasserts itself, or strives to do so, in the noblesse of a king who, as even Macbeth admits, has been meek, clear, and virtuous in his great office (1.7). Thus if Hamlet inherits contamination, Macbeth seems to introduce it. Rapt by witches and wife, his imagination brings forth its monstrous regicidal issue in Duncan's bedchamber, an act that warps the natural orderings of the world (2.4) and even recreates Scotland herself in its image: "It weeps, it bleeds, and each new day a gash / Is added to her wounds" (4.3). But however widespread the consequences of Macbeth's acts, his special brand of evil is in him before it is in the world. As a result, unlike Hamlet, who must deal with evil in the world as well as in himself, Macbeth must come to terms with himself alone.

This sketchy charting of these movements "toward" and "from" meaning in the two plays situates meaning or its absence primarily in the world outside the hero, although of course it is he who perceives it as being or not being out there. However if we situate meaning within the hero, by regarding it as awareness, recognition, or the tragic *anagnorisis,* then a different pattern emerges. Meaning in *Hamlet* then seems not merely the ultimate quasi-religious destination of the hero but his constant attendant on the journey. Meaning, that is, is distributed throughout the play in the form of Hamlet's self-searchings and world-probings, and may even be most present when he registers its apparent absence. *Hamlet,* as someone may have mentioned before, is dominated by the consciousness of the Prince.

Macbeth, however, is dominated by the suppression of consciousness in the usurping King. If Macbeth's killing of Duncan creates a world in the image of that act, it creates Macbeth in its image as well. The murderous deed he brings into being brings him into being also, in a form so repellant that he says "To know my deed, 'twere best not know myself" (2.2). The deed is a violation of Macbeth's "conscience," in the old double sense of "consciousness" as well as "knowledge of right and wrong." Thus the extraordinary conscience revealed by his "If it were done" soliloquy must be deliberately secreted even from himself if he is to continue to function. In his encounter with Banquo's ghost his conscience surfaces again, but that, he assumes, is because he is still "but young in deed" (3.4). After his second meeting with the Witches, as noted earlier, he suppresses conscience altogether, closing the gap between the heart's evil impulse and the hand's blind execution (4.1.146). He now seems perfect tyrant, a murderous reflex action.

In *Hamlet* we are kept conscious not so much of what is happening as of what is not happening—the hero's revenge. Hamlet does his share of acting, both theatrical and actual, yet his and the Ghost's repeated insistence that he is not doing the one large thing he was assigned to do negates his smaller deeds. At the same time this palpable stress on nonaction negates Hamlet's identity, since it tells us not what he is but what he is not—a revenger. But that is only one, albeit the most important, of his non-identities. In the soliloquies that should manifest him to us, he says instead all that he is not: the passionate Player who can weep for Hecuba, the dispassionate Horatio who stoically weeps at nothing, the dutiful obedient son of a murdered father, the compliant son and heir of a murderous stepfather, the lover of Ophelia, the bluff and warlike Fortinbras, or the headlong man of honor Laertes. Most of all he is not what he once was, the Danish courtier-prince whom Castiglione might have called the "expectancy and rose of the fair state, / The glass of fashion and the mold of form." Nor on the other hand is he a madman, except perhaps north-northwest. In a world whose operant principle is "seems" Hamlet cannot "be," not at least until he comes to the graveyard where death "is" and men and maids are "not." There, in the presence of the Great Negative, he can at last affirm his identity: "This is I, / Hamlet, the Dane!"

The action of *Macbeth* is more positive, present, and immediate. The play begins with violence afield and proceeds murderous deed by deed to its bloody end. In keeping with this, its hero is self-constitutive. He shapes his identity in the deeds he performs. Hamlet finds in madplay and wordplay a defiladed cleft between action and inaction, a place where he can be, not do. But the question for Macbeth is not "to be or not to be" but "to act or not to act." Given an either/or moral choice—either kill Duncan and risk the life to come or do not kill him and remain innocent—he chooses evil, and becomes evil, and knows what he has done and has become. His act of innocence after the murder, played for himself as well as for the Scots, fools no one for long, least of all himself. Increasingly as his murderous acts multiply he becomes a known and proclaimed quantity. But not self-proclaimed. Hamlet's "This is I" is a public announcement that marks how far he has come from his early "But I have that within which passeth show." Macbeth's "My way of life / Has fallen into the sear, the yellow leaf" is a private admission that marks how far he has come from his early "I have bought golden opinions from all sorts of people." Yet even at this late point Macbeth seeks his identity in deeds. Whereas Hamlet is content to wait in readiness for a revenge that ultimately comes to him and inflicts a murderous identity upon him, Macbeth, though surrounded like a bear at the stake, cries "Come, wrack! / At least we'll die with harness on our back" and plunges forth to discover who he finally is—mortally guilty or proof against the world.

NEGATION AND INTERPRETATION

Hamlet defers the murderous act that Macbeth finds increasingly easy to perform. That, it seems to me, is because Hamlet finds himself in a far more complex world than Macbeth's, a world that demands action of him but at the same time calls action in doubt. The Ghost's command to kill Claudius requires young Hamlet to become old Hamlet, acting for and as his father. At the same time the conventions of mimetic revenge require that he also become Claudius, his new "father" ("Be as ourself in Denmark"), matching poison with poison, damnation with damnation. Hamlet is too much in the sun/son. Like his favorite figure the pun, which is not either "sun" or "son" but both at once, Hamlet occupies a world that simultaneously is and is not. Such a duck-rabbity world does not invite clearcut choices, nor does Hamlet make any. From action he retreats to "acting," from killing the King to playing mad. Even after he proclaims his identity—"This is I, Hamlet, the Dane!"—he does not sally forth to slay the King crying "Revenge is all!" but says rather "The readiness is all," which is a little like saying "The pre-revenge is all." His readiness assumes that divine providence will bring his revenge to him or, presumably, if not, not. Hamlet is a poststructuralist with an undecidable text. Neither within nor outside himself can he find grounds on which to choose, and so he falls back on faith and impulse ("And praised be rashness for it . . . / and that should learn us / There's a divinity that shapes our ends").

Macbeth on the other hand is something of an existentialist. The Witches may announce that "fair is foul and foul is fair" and issue equivocal prophecies, and Macbeth can murmur that "nothing is but what is not," but when it is time to choose he and especially his Lady readily transform these both/and's into unequivocal either/or's. Instead of Hamlet's "maybe," Macbeth first says "no" to a clearly identified evil and then, prompted by his wife and with eyes averted, whispers "yes." It is a "yes" he pronounces more firmly as he goes on, until he is so habituated to evil that he can let his heart and hand speak for him automatically. Unlike Hamlet, who shies away from choosing until at last death chooses him, Macbeth chooses again and again and pays the price of doing so.

This either/or-ness of Macbeth is consistent with a world whose moral poles are the demonic Witches and the saintly Edward the Confessor. And perhaps Hamlet's both/and-ness is consistent with a Denmark governed by a conscience-stricken usurper, brooded over by a Ghost from a purgatorial neither/nor, and ruled at large by an inscrutable providence. When polymorphic clouds contain camels, weasels, and whales, and when man himself is simultaneously a paragon of animals and a quintessence of dust, no wonder Hamlet's Danish text is hard to read. No

wonder too that Shakespeare's text is hard to read, for like
Elsinore, where everything only "seems," Shakespeare's Globe is
a house of mirrors in which every image is captioned "Not this."
As the history of *Hamlet* criticism attests to, undecidability is built
into the play.

One reason for this undecidability is Shakespeare's reliance on
negation and metadrama. Negation is perhaps most evident near
the end of the Closet Scene when Gertrude asks what she should
do and Hamlet prefaces a vividly seamy description of her betray-
ing him to the bloat King in bed with the words "Not this, by no
means, that I bid you do." Negation thus divides words from
their meanings, which we are told not to register, leaving us with
mere sounds. Or rather we are left in the divide between words
and meanings. In this light one form of metadrama—metatheatrical illusion—is a species of negation. As a visual alienation device,
it says "Not this, by no means, that you seem to see." It negates
the apparent presence of Ophelia, Hamlet, and Elsinore and
leaves us with a boy actor, Richard Burbage, and the stage of the
Globe. Or rather, as with verbal negation, it leaves us in the
divide between the two. For having imagined Hamlet's sordid
scene of Gertrude and Claudius between incestuous sheets, we
cannot unimagine it at the command even of Hamlet's double
negative—any more than we can unimagine Hamlet himself at
Shakespeare's metatheatrical suggestion. In the theater of imagination to see a unicorn is far easier than to unsee one.

In *Macbeth* the speech that is comparable to Hamlet's double
negation occurs when Malcolm tests the potential spy Macduff in
Act 4. Here Malcolm out-Macbeths Macbeth in evils, all self-
attributed, in order to discern evil in Macduff. There is no bottom
to his voluptuousness, no limit to his avarice, no end to his
malice. But when Macduff denounces him, Malcolm rejoices and
then "unspeaks [his] own detraction," abjuring "the taints and
blames [he] laid upon [himself]." In him as in Macduff, evil is
mere illusion. The negative is employed here not to introduce un-
forgettable images to the mind but to erase the obviously false.
This evil is palpably alien to what we already know of the two
men, and hence easily negated, just as evil in England is easily

purified by the touch of the sainted Edward. By contrast, the evil in Scotland is as indelible as the blood on Lady Macbeth's hand; it cannot be negated, only eradicated.

In *Macbeth,* then, negation is genuinely negative. It erases its subject instead of foregrounding it while pretending to erase it as in *Hamlet.* Perhaps that is why negation and metadrama are so much rarer in *Macbeth* than in *Hamlet,* and consequently why it has not presented us with the interpretive problems of the earlier play. Its dramatic mode is positive, a sweeping away of what-is-not in favor of getting to what-is. When Hamlet advises Gertrude *not to do* an evil he then graphically describes, we see that in his world evil is positive, and good is but its pale and bodiless negation. In such times good itself is more illusion than substance— "Assume a virtue, if you have it not"—at best merely habit, custom, the apparel of abstention worn until it seems natural, for "that monster custom"

> who all sense doth eat,
> Of habits devil, is angel yet in this,
> That to the use of actions fair and good
> He likewise gives a frock or livery
> That aptly is put on."   (3.4)

Macbeth reverses this by taking the more orthodox view that evil is the negation of good. Thus in Macbeth's "If it were done" soliloquy good is powerfully imaged as angels trumpeting, the babe pity striding the blast, and cherubim horsed, whereas the evil murder is reduced to an unspecified "it," a nameless deed, clearly a "not good." And to such a deed Macbeth says "No" until Lady Macbeth supplants his images of good with others associated with sexual potency and manhood and babes not striding blasts but with brains dashed out. And to these he says "Yes." And as he proceeds "that monster custom," whom Hamlet invokes to guide Gertrude into the fashion of virtue, gradually "all sense doth eat" in Macbeth until he becomes habituated to murder, though the "frock and livery" he has put on, his "title / Hangs loose about him, like a giant's robe / Upon a dwarfish thief" (5.2).

TIME AND DRAMATIC FORM

As a final point of comparison let me turn now to the issue of time and form. As I mentioned earlier *Hamlet* has a kind of poststructuralist character inasmuch as its hero confronts a deviously undecidable world in which every signifier promises a signified that on inspection turns out to be merely another signifier. His frustrating experience has served as a model for Shakespeare's audiences, struggling as they have over the centuries with his deviously undecidable play. Again, *Hamlet* is poststructuralist, or quasi-Derridean, in its concern for the past, for there is a sense in which Derrida's account of linguistic distinctions is retentive or past-oriented. Concepts like the trace, the supplement, and the remainder presuppose a past that the trace traces, the supplement supplements, and the remainder carries over.[8] From this perspective we can hardly help thinking of the Ghost as a "trace" of Hamlet's father which generates the action of the play by commanding Hamlet—already a genetic trace of his father—to "Remember [him]" by performing an act of revenge that traces Claudius's original murder. Thus Hamlet spends much of his time remembering the past, until near the end when he assumes a readiness that implies anticipation of the future.

Inversely, Macbeth spends much of his time anticipating the future, until near the end when as the failures of the past begin to invade the present he becomes indifferent not merely to the future but to time itself. If we had to call on a philosopher to help us interpret *Macbeth* it might well be Nietzsche, whose theory of signs is protentive or future-oriented in terms of the Will-to-Power. Or instead of Derrida's trace we could rely on his non-concept of "*différance*," not in its synchronic sense of "differing" but in its diachronic sense of "deferring." Instead of a tracelike Ghost of his father crying "Remember me!" Macbeth encounters three witches intoning prophecies about "hereafter." As these prophecies strike Macbeth's ear they add to Derrida's French term "*différance*," with its pun on "differ/defer," the meaning of the English "deference." They not only emphasize how in the normal course of things the gratification of desire must be post-

poned—though Macbeth's will-to-power insists that it be now—
but also how in this case the present, in its poverty, should
humbly defer to a richer future as the bringer of gratification.[9]

To move these issues from Hamlet and Macbeth to *Hamlet* and
Macbeth, we would expect to find that the experiences of the two
heroes somehow reflect the dramatic form in which their experience is depicted. Is the form of *Hamlet* for instance as disregardful
of the future as Hamlet himself? Of course we know from the
Ghost's command that we are witnessing a revenge tragedy and
therefore that a certain future, a climactic act of revenge, is somewhere in the offing. But this future is vague to begin with, and as
the play proceeds, or rather does not proceed, we begin to wonder with the Ghost and Hamlet himself if the revenge will in fact
be consummated. When the revenge does take place, it does not
issue from a plot devised by Hamlet but comes by accident and
improvisation. It is less that Hamlet's revengeful aim has found its
target than that Claudius's plot has gone awry. "Indiscretion,"
Hamlet says, "sometimes serves us well / When our deep plots
do pall" (5.2.8).

This palling of plots within *Hamlet* does not speak auspiciously
for the plot of *Hamlet* itself. Nor does Horatio when he charac-
terizes the play in terms of less than Aristotelean endearment:

> So shall you hear
> Of carnal, bloody, and unnatural acts,
> Of accidental judgments, casual slaughters,
> Of deaths put on by cunning and forced cause,
> And, in the upshot, purposes mistook
> Fallen on the inventors' heads.

All plots seem to fail in *Hamlet,* even Shakespeare's. Why should
that be? Perhaps for the same reason the unity of time "fails" in
the play: because Shakespeare is not interested in it. Creating
a lockstep causal progression, a functionally efficient teleology, a
clean neoclassic act of murder, is simply not his intent. Rather he
is preoccupied with what we might call the retentive mode, with
exploring like Hamlet the magnitude of the dramatic moment,
the richness of its being and not-being, and the range of its poten-

tialities. This magnification of the moment implies a resistance to time's passage, an unwillingness to commit oneself to that functional aspect of the moment that will thrust it into the future. We see this macrocosmically in Hamlet's truancy from his revenge and microcosmically in his reluctance verbally to abandon a thought, as in his "O that this too too sullied flesh would melt, / Thaw, and resolve itself into a dew!" or in his habitual wordplay, which dilates upon meaning at the expense of functional progression. In ways like these, with each dramatic moment lingering out its being as long as possible, the present becomes most fully present as an end in itself, not a means to the future.

Not so in *Macbeth,* which exploits the protentive mode. Here the presence of prophecy announces the presence of pre-plotted action. The future is made explicit so that the audience is not obliged as in *Hamlet* to trail the hero as he wanders toward a terminal act but proceeds by careful directions toward Macbeth's kingship, Banquo's line of kings (Jacobean audiences knew precisely how and when *that* prophecy is fulfilled!), the militant movement of Birnam Wood, and Macbeth's death from a man unnaturally born. All is well conducted. The prophecy about Macbeth's kingship enkindles his ambition and generates the regicidal action that dominates Acts 1 and 2. The prophecy about Banquo's royal offspring enkindles Macbeth's fears and generates the second murder that is featured in Act 3. Then in Act 4 an insecure Macbeth revisits the Witches and hears the prophecies that will govern the remaining action of the play.

Instead of lingering out and magnifying a valued present occasion, the Witches' prophecies and Macbeth's proleptic imaginings assume the poverty of the present and the comparative richness of the future to which it defers. The present is by no means an end in itself but a launching point for the future. Macbeth's asides and soliloquies are not action-quelling explorations of the self, not instances of "thinking too precisely on the event," but incitements to dangerous deeds. The dagger he hallucinates brings a real dagger to his hand, whereas the importuning Ghost—coined, Gertrude claims, by Hamlet's distempered mind—brings only another self-recriminating soliloquy to his lips a few scenes later

(4.4). When Macbeth says "Now o'er the one half-world / Nature seems dead" he is not memorializing the moment but imaginatively transforming it into a scene of future killing.

In *Hamlet* "presence," which takes the form of a maximal experiencing of both what is and what is not, is *in* the present, or at least it is sought for there by both Shakespeare and Hamlet as each seeks to exhaust the verbal, theatrical, and imaginative possibilities of the moment. This maximizing of the present occasion implies that Shakespeare and his hero repeatedly attempt to spatialize time by retarding the flow of events. But of course such attempts are futile, belying as they do the nature of drama as a temporal performance. Resist it as they will, Hamlet's dilatory madplay and wordplay and Shakespeare's stageplay must all continue on if they are ever to end. Time, death, and the Gravemaker are in readiness for their roles. So at last is Hamlet.

On the other hand "presence" in *Macbeth,* which takes the illusory form of satisfied desire, lies vaguely in the future. For Macbeth himself presence is the satisfaction of ambitious yearnings; for the audience it is the satisfaction of formal expectations. Shakespeare is kinder to his audience in this respect than he is to his hero, since Macbeth's desire is never satisfied. No sooner is he on the throne than he grows restless, for "To be thus is nothing, / But to be safely thus" (3.1.47). So Banquo must die, else he will be "father to a line of kings" (3.1.59). And so Banquo dies. But Fleance escapes, and Macbeth, who "had else been perfect" (3.4.21), suffers his "fit" again. Ultimately Macbeth achieves a state of indifference in which desire has subsided not from satisfaction but from enervation. Presence arrives in abundance to a Macbeth replete but not fulfilled:

> I have supped full with horrors;
> Direness, familiar to my slaughterous thoughts,
> Cannot once start me.   (5.5.13)

For the audience, however, the plot of the play guarantees more authentic satisfactions as cause leads to effect, and motive issues in action. The prophecies, which are merely the most obvious form of dramatic anticipation, are structural promises given his audience by the playwright, and they are all kept. Macbeth's kingship, the march of Birnam Wood to Dunsinane, the killing of Macbeth by one "not of woman born"—these are fully meaningful not in themselves but as "that which was predicted." Thus the play is not only protentive but retentive; it remembers its past and the obligations incurred there, and in fulfilling those obligations it creates dramatic form. This making and keeping of promises by the playwright imparts order to theatrical time, enabling the play to transcend Macbeth's final conception of life as an entropic drama rendered absurd by the petty pace of indistinguishable tomorrows. More than that, it imparts meaning. For Macbeth this drama of life signifies "nothing." Literally, it seems, it has no signified. This is in keeping with the fact that Macbeth's pursuit of desire is like the postmodern view of the signifier's pursuit of the signified, which on attainment turns into merely another signifier, another meaningless "tomorrow." But that is not the experience of the audience, which as I have said finds gratification in Shakespeare's conversion of ambitious desire on Macbeth's part into prophetic form in *Macbeth,* so that the climax of the play is not undifferentiated happenings but predicted events whose verbal mysteriousness becomes comprehensible in action. The endless current of signification is at least momentarily, meaningfully arrested in time by Shakespeare's fulfilling form.

Two

Done and Undone:

Macbeth as Tragic Action

amlet is a play about the preconditions of action—the marshallings of motive, the exploratory coming to terms with scene, the final poising of mind in a state of "readiness" from which the hero's revenge can issue. Thus what follows from Hamlet's act—Denmark's future under (we assume) the enigmatic Fortinbras—is left unexamined: "The rest is silence." *King Lear* on the other hand is a play about the consequences of action—the dizzying descent toward nothingness, the handy-dandy inversion of identities and values, the mad-blind groping for orders of recovery. *Hamlet* rises to action, *Lear* falls from action. Thus what leads up to Lear's act—his motives for dividing his kingdom, his reasons for staging the competition in praise—is left as unexamined as what follows from Hamlet's. All that came before seems blank. What is done in *Lear* is done swiftly; what follows is explored at painful length.

Considered as the dramatic heir of these earlier tragedies, *Macbeth* seems to inherit something of *Hamlet*'s concern for "presequences" and perhaps even more of *Lear*'s obsession with consequences. Thus we see the tragic act both before its performance, as it takes shape in the hero's imagination, and afterwards too, as its fatal effects ramify within him and his world. In no other play does Shakespeare address himself so pervasively to tragic action—to the tragic action of his hero and to the tragic action that is his play. In no other play do the words "do," "done," and "deed" appear so often or so centrally. *Macbeth* almost seems to become a tragedy by taking for its subject the actional essence of the tragic genre. And yet if the play is about action, about what is done, it is also about not-action, what is undone.

"Done and undone" seems in keeping with a play that begins with witches telling of battles lost and won and of how fair is foul and foul fair. It suggests that Shakespeare has recast Aristotle's concept of tragic action in the mode of oracular equivocation. For Aristotle is most soberly unequivocal about tragic action. He says that tragedy is the mimesis of "an action that is whole and complete" and that for an action to be whole and complete it must possess a beginning, a middle, and an end. Then to be sure we are quite clear about it he defines a beginning as that which does not follow something else but after which something follows, and an end as that which *does* follow something else but after which nothing follows, and a middle as . . . Well, at any rate the action should be whole and yet properly parted (*Poetics,* 1450b).

At first glance Shakespeare seems to have observed these precepts about tragic action more strictly than the Attic playwrights from whom Aristotle derived them. For instance whereas *Oedipus Tyrannus* commences with its prophecies already fulfilled and its story well advanced, *Macbeth* begins at the beginning and presents its tragic action in its entirety. Thus we witness the fall of Shakespeare's hero from the earliest moment when he stands at cliff's edge debating whether or not to leap, whereas when we first see Oedipus he is already in mid-descent, perhaps four-fifths of the way down—anyhow at a point where there are fewer options below him than above him. Of course that is so typically the case that most classical tragedies look like merely expanded last acts of Shakespearean plays. Moreover, not only has Sophocles' play already begun when we enter, but it has not yet ended when we leave: still to come are *Oedipus at Colonus* and at a further reach of consequence, *Antigone*. But the action of *Macbeth* is complete. Its prophecies are issued and fulfilled on stage; it has a proper beginning and a proper ending.[1]

Or has it? Where after all does *Macbeth* begin?

The answer would seem obvious: it begins where all plays begin, with its opening scene, its opening speech. However, the opening scene of *Macbeth* is rather curious insofar as it seems designed to announce that it is not a beginning. It is not a beginning on the one hand because its action has already begun. The Witches will meet again, they say, "When the hurly-burly's done." That is, we enter the play not at the beginning but in mid-hurly-burly, before the battle's lost and won. That is not remarkable. Under the classical heading of *in medias res* it is a perfectly respectable way to (not)-begin a play.

So the play does not begin where it seems to begin because it has already begun. On the other hand it has not yet begun where it seems to begin. The first line of the Witches—"When shall we three meet again?"—is not a beginning but a postponement of a beginning. We are privy to a witchy meeting whose only evident function is to announce a future meeting—

> Where the place?
>
>   Upon the heath.
>
> There to meet with Macbeth.

We could call this the Witches' first prophecy. It has the somewhat disconcerting effect of effacing not only this opening scene but the battle-scene that follows it, which the audience sees through or beyond in anticipation of the promised encounter in Scene 3. It is as though we are looking at a painting in which one figure negates itself by pointing to a second which in turn points to a third. (This self-annulling aspect of the scene as an action mirrors the self-annullments of its verse—the semantic cross-cancellation of fair and foul and won and lost—and of the Witches' appearance as men-women.) Not until Macbeth and Banquo accost the Witches on the heath do we feel that the action of the play has actually begun, especially since this later meeting features prophecies and proleptic imaginings that thrust the action toward the future. And yet this belated beginning is also a kind of ending inasmuch as it fulfills the Witches' promise in Scene 1 to meet with Macbeth upon the heath. Where actions and plays begin and end becomes a bit problematic.

Instead of a beginning, then, we have an unbeginning. Which makes us wonder of course if we also have an unending. At first glance it would seem not. Instead we seem to have a decisive closure of action signalled by the clear-cut victory of the forces under Malcolm and by the entrance of Macduff with the tyrant's head on his pike. "The time is free," Macduff proclaims. Yet we have leave to doubt if it is more than temporarily free. For his fixing of Macbeth's head upon his pike cannot help reminding us that just so did Macbeth "[fix McDonwald's] head upon [the] battlements" after an earlier battle (1.2.22). Like the early Macbeth, Macduff has fought loyally for the rightful king and killed a rebel. Surely he has "bought golden opinions from all sorts of people" and will soon be honored by young Malcolm (1.7.33). Indeed the parallels are so pronounced that we might well wonder if as Macduff returns home across the heath he will suddenly rein in, murmuring "What are these / So withered and so wild in their attire?" For now, after all, is "when the hurly-burly's done, / When the battle's lost and won"—the time when the Witches seek out victors.

To suggest, however, that *Macbeth* is not yet done, that its ending is an unending, we need hardly claim that Macduff is literally about to embark on a career of murder and usurpation. The very cyclicism of time and nature that brings sterility and symbolic old age to a hibernal Macbeth (5.3.24), that brings Birnam Wood to Dunsinane as in a May festival, and that brings ritual purgation and regeneration to Scotland implies that in the great revolution of things there is no final end, only a return to beginnings. Thus when Malcolm speaks of what "would be newly planted with the time" (5.8.66)—echoing his father's words to Macbeth, "I have begun to plant thee, and will labor / To make thee full of growing" (1.4.28)—we are invited to suspect that what is newly planted may be not merely peace and fellowship but the seeds of a future which, had we the gift of prophecy, might look very much like the past.[2]

To an unbeginning, then, perhaps we can add an unending—an unending that runs by a commodious vicus of recirculation back into that unbeginning, somewhat as the ending of *Macbeth* in the theater today will return to its beginning at tomorrow's performance. Tragic deeds in Scotland and tragic acts in the Globe both seem in perpetual pursuit of themselves, in an endless state of un-closure. If there is some likeness between tragic deeds and dra-matic acts, then tracing out the implication of the word "done" and its opposite "undone" may put us in a position to see it more clearly. Let us turn to such doings.

"IF IT WERE DONE"

Action, Aristotle implies, is the soul of plot, and plot is the soul of tragedy. He might have added that action is the soul of the tragic hero too. For if there is one trait shared by tragic heroes it is that they are not passive but active characters. Whether they act freely or upon compulsion and insinuation, with foreknowledge or in ignorance, by accident or design, for good or ill, tragic heroes are alike in that they *do* act—and suffer the consequences of their action. The more sentient they are, the more likely they are to pause warily before the complexities and consequences of action, as Hamlet does, or even as Macbeth does—for Macbeth is never more sensitive to the mysteries of action than in those arrested moments before the deed when he persuades himself not to do it.

In the famous soliloquy of Act 1, Scene 7, Macbeth's imagina-tion dwells on the question of where an act ends. In the double sense of "done," will the murderous deed be completed when it is performed? Will the assassination trammel up the consequence? One of the first consequences of the deed is its effect on the doer even before it is done. Perhaps nowhere else in literature are we more reminded that a word is not merely a unit in a message but a verbal act, a manifestation of self. Thus the first four words of Macbeth's soliloquy, though barren of figuration, are immensely implicative of his state of mind, of what his wife would dismiss as his unmanly fastidiousness about murder. What for her would be a straightforward "When I kill Duncan" becomes for her husband "If it were done."

Macbeth's employment of "if" signals his entrance into a world of subjunctive possibilities where the murderous-minded may indulge themselves without fear of indictment. The pronoun "it" leaves undefined a deed his conscience forbids him to name. The passive "were" subtracts a human subject from the lethal affair as though the deed could create itself. And the tense of "done" transforms a fearsome future into a safely completed past.[3] The remainder of the line, with its incantatory repetition of "done"— "If it were done when 'tis done, then 'twere well / It were done quickly"—suggests the futility of Macbeth's desire to have the deed concluded, for the word goes on tolling as relentlessly within the line as the deed itself will do in Scotland. And yet the soliloquy itself does not end. As Macbeth speaks of "vaulting ambition, which o'erleaps itself / And falls on the other . . ." Lady Macbeth enters, and he says "How now, what news?" "Vaulting ambition" is appropriately her cue to appear.

The soliloquy as a whole reveals a Macbeth who possesses at least the illusion of free will. I say "illusion" because there is a sense in which the murder of Duncan took place the moment Macbeth heard the prophecies on the heath and gave way to "horrible imaginings," to "my thought, whose murder yet is but fantastical" (1.3). Macbeth's "yet" suggests a murder that both is and is not inevitable ("The deed may be fantastical now, but it will be actual later" but also "It is after all merely fantastical, therefore harmless"), and thus admirably sums up the ambiguous fusion of destiny and freedom in Macbeth at this moment. It is the freedom that is dominant during the "If it were done" speech, since in it Macbeth weighs his options and persuades himself to abandon the plot. That a sense of freedom should accompany this imaginative soliloquy is fitting because it is in acts of imagining that we feel most immediately autonomous.[4] We all have moments when we cannot remember, reason, or even perceive, but we can almost invariably imagine at will. We simply intend the image and it is there regardless of time, space, the laws of logic or nature. Imagining is easy; not-imagining is hard.

If imagination demonstrates its freedom by transporting us out of our immediate world, Macbeth's next soliloquy seems somewhat perverse, since it is designed to deprive him of freedom by inserting him and his deed into the world. Bent now on murder he imagines an airborne dagger marshalling him the way he was going. Then he fashions by a kind of word magic a diabolical scene ("Now o'er the one half-world" etc.) in which regicide is not only possible but obligatory. And finally he transforms the bell that calls him to bed into an invitation to send Duncan to heaven or to hell. The whole speech marvelously illustrates the workings of a self-protective consciousness as it projects inner impulses outward to create a behavioristic world to whose stimuli it can then react. In a speeded-up version of operant conditioning, Macbeth—drawn by the dagger, instructed by dead nature, and called by the bell—renders himself as much a victim of the murderous act as Duncan. For the audience, what Macbeth does to the sleeping King becomes almost secondary to what Macbeth does to Macbeth.

This victimization of Macbeth by his self-projected scene is reflected in the plight of the actor who plays Macbeth. Whereas in the "If it were done" speech Macbeth's imagination detaches him from his immediate scene in the castle so that he seems merely a voice issuing from nowhere, in this soliloquy he is palpably present and implicated in his world. He sees an imaginary dagger, he clutches at it, he draws a real dagger, he acknowledges darkness and the firm-set earth, he treads on stone, he hears a bell, and he makes his ominous departure. His fantasies are thoroughly threaded into the fabric of sensory reality, even as he is merging into the malevolence of his created world, even as the subjunctive pastness of his deed as formulated earlier passes into the present indicative: "I go, and it is done." This ritualization of murder converts Macbeth into a player who must act in accordance with his part. By the same token the actor who plays Macbeth must comply with the "stage directions" written into the soliloquy by seeing an imaginary dagger, by drawing a real one, and so on.

The player is as compelled to act in his realm as Macbeth is in his.

Then the deed is done, and Macbeth's worst fears begin to be realized. For what is performed is by no means concluded. "But wherefore could not I pronounce 'Amen'?" Wherefore indeed? Not merely because he has passed beyond God's grace but because the deed is not yet done; that is why "Amen" sticks in his throat. The nature of action and especially of tragic action is that it generates reaction, and the first reaction takes place within the agent. The man who brings an act into being is in turn brought into being by his act: by their deeds you shall know them. That is why Macbeth sought to imagine a deed without a doer, an act that would erase the actor by converting him into a personified response. That is why he imagined a diabolical world in which a diabolical act would disappear through protective coloration. Most criminals hope to succeed by concealing their identities from others afterwards. Macbeth conceals his identity from himself in order to perform the deed. Then, to live with what he has done, he must erase his knowledge of himself: "To know my deed, 'twere best not know myself." Or as Robert B. Heilman puts it, "Macbeth murders not only Duncan but a part of himself."[5]

Macbeth's inability to say "Amen" to the deed is prophetic. For as the word "done" tolls three times within his famous line, so his deed tolls thrice in Scotland. I mean that the murder of Duncan, of Banquo, and of Macduff's family is in a sense one deed tripled. Not that the three murders directly resemble one another but that the second is a displaced version of the first, and the third a displaced version of both. By the same token the second is an attempt to perfect the first, and the third is an attempt to complete the second. Macbeth is like a child who lies once, and then is compelled to repeat the lie with variations to prevent its discovery. Thus when Lady Macbeth says of Duncan's murder "What's done is done," Macbeth replies "We have scorched the snake, not killed it. / She'll close and be herself" (3.2.14). The scorched snake survives—which seems to mean that Duncan in some sense still survives. If so, how will killing Banquo and Fleance, as Macbeth now intends, complete the killing of Duncan, who is already in his grave? And why, when Fleance escapes and Banquo's ghost returns, is Macbeth, learning also of the flight of Macduff, anxious to destroy Macduff's "line"?

> Seize upon Fife, give to the edge o' the sword
> His wife, his babes, and all unfortunate souls
> That trace him in his line.   (4.1.151)

Banquo must be killed, Macbeth says, lest he become "father to a line of kings" (3.1.59), and Macbeth's henchmen must make sure to destroy all those "that trace [Macduff] in his line." Macbeth, it seems, is obsessively line-conscious, and he is right to be so, since he is himself caught in the irreversible flow of action. In a linear form—a sentence, a play, a temporal series of acts, history itself—the only way to return to an earlier point is by continuing onward. But this attempt to regress progressively inevitably opens the temporal gap one wants to close, as Tristram Shandy discovers by living 364 times faster than he can write about his living. In Macbeth's case, this means that to complete his first act he must proceed to further acts that are themselves cursed with incompleteness. Each effort to repair a prior act only emphasizes its deficiency. Ultimately, realizing the infinite regress he has been caught up in, he says

> I am in blood
> Stepped in so far that, should I wade no more,
> Returning were as tedious as go o'er.

> (3.4.137)

Macbeth is forced into his curious mode of regressive progression by virtue of the unending nature of action. The murder of Duncan remains ominously undone because Duncan's sons escape, who had they stayed "should [have found] / What 'twere to kill a father" (3.6.20). The perfect act, the deed fully "done," would have killed Duncan and then his sons as purported parricides. But the sons live, and Duncan lives in them. So, contrary to Lady Macbeth, what's done is not done; the dead King lives symbolically, and potential future kings live in fact. Let us then kill future kings, if not Duncan's sons, then Banquo's. For "in [Banquo's] royalty of nature / Reigns that which would be feared" (3.1.49). The muted notion that Duncan lives on in

Malcolm and Donalbain becomes explicit in Banquo and his "line." Banquo, in whom Macbeth's fears stick deep, will not be dead unless Fleance dies too. But this deed also remains undone when the aptly named Fleance flees. Macbeth can kill fathers but not sons, the past but not the future. Let us then kill off the future randomly, if not Banquo's line, then Macduff's. But time "anticipat'st [Macbeth's] dread exploits" (4.1.144), and Macduff escapes. Macbeth finally kills a son, but it is the wrong son, neither Malcolm nor Fleance.

Macduff escapes before the deed, Fleance escapes during it, and Malcolm and Donalbain escape after it, as though Shakespeare dissolves the structure of action from every temporal angle, rendering it amorphous and uncontained, anything but the bounded form our reifying imaginations fabricate when like Macbeth we are fearful of consequences and want something secure to hold to. For if a man is defined by his deeds, and his deeds cannot be defined, who or what does that make him? If his act is never done, his identity never crystalizes. His very doing is his undoing.

Moreover, the deed that is undone in time is undone in space as well. In life very few acts alter their physical scene, the environment being most sensitive to what is done to it but not to what is done within it. Indeed its indifference to acts is notorious—blood spurts and bodies pile up, but the grass grows and the cattle graze on. Not in Scotland, however. The murder of Duncan reverberates in the highlands and even incarnadines the seas. It transforms Inverness, where to the newly arrived Duncan "heaven's breath [smelled] wooingly," into the Porter's hell. So sensitive is nature that it even allegorizes the deed, causing Macbeth-like owls to hawk presumptuously at royal falcons, and horses to eat each other. And in sympathy for the eclipsed sun king, it causes darkness to entomb the earth, as Lady Macbeth had predicted when told that Duncan would go hence "tomorrow": "O never shall sun that morrow see."

"I HAVE DONE THE DEED"

I have been tracing the ways in which the word "done" in the first line of Macbeth's famous soliloquy ramifies throughout the play as a kind of "undoing," an act that fails to achieve completion or

take form within definable limits. In the present section I want to
suggest that the murderous deed is undone in another sense, because it is done metaphorically. Let us begin with Macbeth's use
of an odd similitude. It occurs in his self-hypnotizing speech just
before the murder as he moves toward Duncan's chambers imagining a world of darkness and evil:

> Now 'er the one half-world
> Nature seems dead, and wicked dreams abuse
> The curtained sleep; witchcraft celebrates
> Pale Hecate's offerings, and withered murder,
> Alarumed by his sentinel, the wolf,
> Whose howl's his watch, thus with his stealthy pace,
> With Tarquin's ravishing strides, towards his design
> Moves like a ghost.   (2.1)

As he imagines an external scene fit for murderous action,
Macbeth also imagines a suitable agent for that act—"withered
murder." Then this murderous personification moves toward its
design like a ghost, marshalling Macbeth the way that he was
going. In the next lines—"Thou sure and first-set earth, / Hear
not my steps, which way they walk"—Macbeth assimilates the
ghostly, Tarquin-striding figure of murder into his own ominous
movement toward Duncan. Macbeth's figuring himself as in-
carnate murder should not, however, give us pause, so much as
his likening himself to Tarquin. For to imagine Macbeth in the
role of, say, Richard Crookback stalking Henry VI would seem
appropriate enough, albeit anachronistic, but for him to appear as
Tarquin lasciviously bent on Lucrece is a bit disconcerting. Yet
Shakespeare seems intent on this rapacious image. Thus when
Macbeth emerges from the chamber to announce "I have done the
deed," Shakespeare can hardly expect his audience not to register
the familiar sexual sense of that expression. Especially not when
he has strewn his play with such terms as "done," "deed," and
"do," and even provided a Witch who ambitiously asserts "I'll
do, I'll do, and I'll do" (1.3.10).

After all, not many bawdy meanings sidle past Shakespeare
without drawing his amused glance—and surely not one so popu-

lar as to be cited in both Tavener's *Proverbs* and the *Oxford Diction-
ary of Proverbs* as a commonplace of the time: "the thynge that is
done cannot be undone." His audience may not remember the
following exchange between Aaron and Tamora's sons in *Titus
Andronicus* (4.2.73 ff.)—

> Villain, what has thou done?
> That which thou canst not undo.
> Thou has undone our mother.
> Villain, I have done thy mother

—but who can forget the aptly-named Mistress Overdone in
Measure for Measure? Or, to seduce the bawdy meaning into the
tenebrous milieu of *Macbeth,* we can note the reference in *Pericles*
to "the deed of darkness" (4.6.32) and Rosalind's advice in *Love's
Labour's Lost,* "Look, what you do, you do it still in the dark"
(5.2.24).

In light of all this, we may well wonder just what Macbeth is up
to in the King's chambers.

To forestall evil imaginings: I mean merely that in depicting the
murder of Duncan Shakespeare inverts his usual figurative practice of likening the sexual act to various acts of violence. This
practice, though hardly unique to Shakespeare, is noted by Eric
Partridge, who after listing a page or so of Shakespearean verbs of
coition writes "The sadism or, rather less cruelly, the brutality or,
less brutally, the 'manly' roughness of so many male terms for 'to
copulate (with)' is as noticeable as the submissiveness, or even the
fatalism, of many of the female verbs."[6] At this point in *Macbeth,*
instead of the sexual act being brutal, the brutal murder is sexual.
But only metaphorically sexual. And sexual in reference not to
Macbeth and Duncan but to Macbeth and Lady Macbeth. That is
to say, the murder of Duncan is a metaphorically displaced act of
copulation between Lord and Lady Macbeth.

Let us go back a bit and see how this is prepared for. To begin
with, I suppose one would have to take note of Lady Macbeth's
unsexing herself "here." Although that might amusingly suggest
that any further copulation on her part would necessarily be metaphoric, it also illustrates the equation of sex and violence whereby

the murder can become a substitute for the sexual act, all the Lady's libidinous energies being rechanneled into violence. And Macbeth's energies, are they also metaphorically sexual? Well, for one thing, the time is right: it is his first night home after a military campaign, and he has ridden back so rapidly that Duncan says "his great love, sharp as his spur, hath holp him / To his home before us" (1.6). So phrased, Macbeth's "love" is ambiguous enough to refer either to Lady Macbeth, whom he spurs lustily home to meet, or to Duncan, whom he dutifully precedes in order to prepare a welcome. At any rate this "love" that is "sharp as a spur" is dulled somewhat when, at the end of his great soliloquy, he admits in suggestive terms:

> I have no spur
> To prick the sides of my intent, but only
> Vaulting ambition, which o'erleaps itself
> And falls on the other.

This lagging of passion causes his lady to upbraid him for wishing "to proceed no further in this business." In doing so she introduces a new metaphoric turn by stressing the effects of drink on ambitious/sexual impulse:

> Was the hope drunk
> Wherein you dressed yourself? Hath it slept since?
> And wakes it now, to look so green and pale
> At what it did so freely? From this time
> Such I account thy love. Art thou afeard
> To be the same in thine own act and valor
> As thou art in desire?   (1.7.36)

Various critics have taken note of the sexual overtones here, as the Lady makes her Lord's virility dependent on his willingness to murder Duncan.[7] At this point his unrealized, murderous hopes seem as unperformable and impotent as a drunkard's brags. The metaphor of lust, subdued in her terms "love," "act," and "desire," becomes explicitly associated with drunkenness after the deed has been done, when the Porter tells Macduff that drink is an "equivocator with lechery" because "it provokes the desire, but it takes away the performance" (2.3.28). But the alcoholic impotence Lady Macbeth attributes to her husband disappears immediately before the murder. Macbeth has told his servant, "Go bid thy mistress, when my drink is ready, / She strike upon the bell" (2.1.32), but when the bell does ring, the "drink" it symbolizes arouses Macbeth's murderous desire without in the least taking away the performance: "I go, and it is done; the bell invites me."

This association of drink, lust, and murderous ambition is reaffirmed in the following scene when Lady Macbeth emerges from Duncan's chamber to say of the grooms, "That which hath made them drunk hath made me bold; / What hath quenched them hath given me fire" (2.2.1). This is surely a strange, perverted moment, with Macbeth "about it" in the bedchamber and the emboldened Lady Macbeth physically outside listening but imaginatively inside "doing the deed" with her husband. Then Macbeth comes forth to announce "I have done the deed," and she cries "My husband!" and the two of them conduct their harrowing aftertalk. Later, Macbeth removes his clothes, dons a nightgown, and pretends to have been roused from bed by the arrival of Macduff.

This imagery of sexual impotence, stimulation, and performance constitutes an erotic metaphor for murder, a kind of intermittent flashing onto the regicidal screen of a subliminal image of the sexual act. The effect is to confuse the two deeds in the audience's imagination and thus to "undo" the murder—that is, to contaminate its purity as an Aristotelean action that is whole and complete in itself. If the deed is both a murder and a sexual act, then it is neither a murder nor a sexual act but something monstrous and unnameable. In the following sections I'll make further feints toward naming the deed, but for the moment let me regard it merely in one aspect, as a murderous substitute for coition between Lord and Lady Macbeth.[8] From that perspective, what should have been a natural and loving act performed in the interests of procreation has been transformed into an act of unnatural and cruel destruction—a deed of uncreation by a woman who has invoked spirits to unsex her and by a man who has invoked the powers of fantasy to reduce himself to an engine of annihilation. Yet at the same time this uncreating act is procreative, inasmuch as its destructiveness multiplies throughout Scotland and within Macbeth.

Shakespeare's erotic metaphor is not as far-fetched as it might seem; for tragic actions, even less murderous tragic actions than this, can be likened to the sexual act which may or may not, as the Victorians said, "have consequences." Before the advent of contraception, the deed of darkness was a concrete corporeal reminder that action is uncertain and that men must take responsibility for what they do without knowing just what it is they do. For the actor is defined by his act, and his act is defined by its issue. At the center of all action is a germinal darkness, a field of potentialities in which only witches can tell which grains will grow and which will not.[9]

Macbeth knows this from the beginning. He fears the potency of action, its capacity to generate consequences, "teach bloody instructions," and leave indelible bloodstains. Thus he longs for a murder that is an end in itself, like the act of lust in Sonnet 129 that begets nothing and hence is but an expense of spirit in a waste of shame. But Macbeth's act, however shameful, is not sterile. It generates unforeseeable reactions in himself and his world. His own inner recoil from the act afterwards is mirrored outwardly by the flight of Duncan's sons from Inverness and the gathering of retributive armies in England. Moreover, the act propagates subsequent acts which have as their aim the murder of offspring, as though Macbeth were seeking Cronus-like to devour the progeny of his own deed. Thus it is appropriate that as he prepares to assault Macduff's children he says "the firstlings of my heart shall be / The firstlings of my hand" (4.1.145), since "firstlings" can mean "firstborn young" as well as "first results."[10] As part of this barrening of Scotland, even his own children are figuratively destroyed by his wife, who dashes their brains out with brutal rhetoric if not in fact (1.7.55).

As Macbeth's deed multiplies, radiating sterility and death, it strikes ultimately at all things that yield life and order. Thus it leads suggestively back to the heath where he interrupts the Witches performing "a deed without a name"—the stewing up of dismembered creatures to create a charm (4.1)—and demands answers from them at any cost,

> though the treasure
> Of nature's germains tumble all together,
> Even till destruction sicken.

At this point his uncreating deed of darkness, joining theirs, finds its furthest symbolic reach, adumbrating at the most fundamental level something like a return to original chaos and old night.

"NOTHING IS BUT WHAT IS NOT"

We have regarded the deed as undone, first, insofar as it is incomplete and endless and, second, insofar as its conceptual integrity is deconstructed by erotic metaphors, leaving us with an unnameable and somewhat monstrous act. The erotic metaphor—bluntly, "murder is coition"—would have been relatively harmless had the murder been staged. Then an imagined sexual act would have been erased by the visual fact of murder. As it is, however, Shakespeare's "unstaging" of the deed allows the erotic metaphor a kind of equal play in our imaginations with a murder that is itself only imagined. Let us then look at this third sense in which the deed is undone. Why, we might well wonder, should Shakespeare keep the deed hidden from his audience in the Globe?

At the end of Act 2, Scene 1, Macbeth exits with the words "Hear it not, Duncan, for it is a knell / That summons thee to heaven or to hell," and midway in the following scene he enters again saying "I have done the deed." In the long caesura between these two speeches we are given, instead of the deed itself, a speech by Lady Macbeth as she stands outside Duncan's rooms:

> That which hath made them drunk hath made me
>   bold;
> What hath quenched them hath given me fire.
>   Hark! Peace!
> It was the owl that shrieked, the fatal bellman,
> Which gives the sternest good-night. He is about it.
> The doors are open, and the surfeited grooms
> Do mock their charge with snores. I have drugged
>   their possets,

> That death and nature do contend about them
> Whether they live or die.
>
> MACBETH [*Within*] Who's there? What, ho!
>
> LADY M.   Alack, I am afraid they have awaked,
> And 'tis not done. The attempt and not the deed
> Confounds us. Hark! I laid their daggers ready,
> He could not miss them. Had he not resembled
> My father as he slept, I had done it.

A strange thing, it seems, to omit so great an act. After all, when Henry VI, Richard II, and Caesar went to it, or when Hamlet took his revenge, or even when Gloucester's eyes were ground out, Shakespeare made certain his audience was witness to the deed. For that matter, later in *Macbeth* we are privy to the hacking down of Banquo, the stabbing of Macduff's son, and the bloody death of Macbeth himself. Surely neither personal squeamishness nor a respect for classical decorum restrains Shakespeare from exhibiting Macbeth's act. What does? Well, there are the supposed outside reasons. Shakespeare cannot dramatize an act of regicide so soon after the Gunpowder Plot—especially not before the king who was the object of that plot, and more especially not when the playwright himself has known some of the Catholic conspirators since childhood.[11] After all, only a few years ago his company was haled before the authorities to account for that private performance of *Richard II* for Essex's followers. In fact after the Gunpowder Plot, and except for Macbeth himself, Shakespeare lets no kings be killed on stage, though he had blithely done away with Henry VI, Richard III, Richard II, Julius Caesar, and Claudius before then (at a time presumably when killing kings was permissible but killing queens was to be most studiously avoided).

The inside reasons are more interesting. One arises from Shakespeare's having chosen the particularly difficult task of casting a criminal in the role of tragic hero.[12] As a result Macbeth the criminal must perform an act of unquestioned evil while Macbeth the tragic hero somehow retains the sympathy of the audience. In the interests of evil, then, let the murder be thoroughly premeditated, as indeed it is. In the interests of audience sympathy, however, let it be more than premeditated—let it be passionately imagined. How will this help the hero? By suggesting that in a sense the murder is not premeditated at all.

Some characters choose murder. Electra, Richard III, Beatrice Cenci, Raskolnikov, Camus's Caligula, all more or less rationally weigh risk against gain and select the murderous option. Whether we admire or deplore their decision, we understand their reasons for making it. On the heath, however, Macbeth does not reckon profit against loss and conclude that murdering Duncan is his likeliest route to kingship. In fact, apart from a passing reference to the "imperial theme" he scarcely mentions kingship. When he writes to his wife about the prophecies it is so she can rejoice not in his auspicious fortunes but in "what greatness is promised *thee*." Not that Macbeth is oblivious to the kingship, the appeal of which goes without saying. But even so, the murder seems less a means to kingship than an object of intrinsic fascination, almost an end in itself, as though to kill the King were automatically to become a king. Hence Macbeth does not imagine *beyond* the act, even in practical terms, which may be why he makes such tactical errors as killing the guards and letting Duncan's sons escape. Instead, the murder itself takes total possession of his mind. Not a killing—he is, after all, a veteran killer on the battlefield—but a murder. And not just any murder, but regicide, a deed that so exceeds all others that it cannot be named—especially on the stage of the Globe with King James a likely member of the audience. [13]

What I am suggesting is that Macbeth "falls in evil" as other men fall in love. The murder of Duncan happens to him the way Juliet happens to Romeo. Whether it is moral, rational, or practical is irrelevant. Our attempts to uncover "real" motives for Macbeth may be as beside the point as they are for Iago. Not that we ever uncover real motives anyhow. Finding the origin of an act is no easier than finding its end, and Macbeth testifies to the impossibility of that. Why does Iago act as he does? He has reasons, he says, but few find them persuasive—he protests too much. So Coleridge says he is a case of motiveless malignity, which makes a point but also substitutes eloquence for explanation. So Bernard Spivack says our question is misdirected, that we should not ask why Iago does evil in Venice but why Shakespeare makes him do evil in the Globe.[14] To which Shakespeare would presumably reply "Because he is a stage villain, and stage villains, as Coleridge points out, have no motives; they are artists in evil. They enjoy plotting for its own sake. I rather enjoy it too, being after all an artist in evil myself."

Iago, then, is explained by the role he plays—a sensible reminder that we are dealing not with life but theater, yet at the same time not altogether satisfying either, inasmuch as it is theater instinct with life. If Elizabethan audiences ever said to themselves "Iago is evil because he is a stage villain like Aaron the Moor, Richard Crookback, and Don John," they would have known, as we do, that that is only half an answer. Stage villainy implies real villainy; it answers, however obliquely, to something in life. When those mythical creatures, the Elizabethans, went hunting for the real life source of evil motives, voicing the child's repeated "Why?" to every seeming answer, they worked their way past nature and humors psychology and the various venial and deadly sins until they came to that unmoved first mover, the Devil, the "real life" source of the Vice who was in turn the theatrical source of the villain. Behind Iago is the Vice, and behind the Vice is the ancient common enemy of man, hoofed and tailed and somewhat hairy of cheek. Of course Iago lacks hoofs, as Othello notes, yet when Othello stabs him with the words "If that thou be'st a devil, I cannot kill thee," he gives a devilish reply, "I bleed, sir, but not killed." Thus the arbitrary origin of Iago's evil seems a coalescence of the theatrical and the theological—the Vice in the Globe, the Devil in Venice.[15]

Macbeth, however, is neither a Vice nor a villain; he is a criminal—a criminal who is also a tragic hero. That means he has ties with Othello as well as with Iago. If these two combine in Macbeth in some degree, they first combine in Othello. It is a case of demonic possession. Othello is possessed by the devil in Iago at the end of Act 3, Scene 4 when the two of them kneel in a mock wedding ceremony and pledge their troth to evil, after which Othello says "Now art thou my lieutenant" and Iago chillingly replies "I am your own forever." So wooed and won, Othello from this point on could aptly take Iago's words for his own: "I

am not what I am." In *Macbeth* a comparable moment occurs
when the hero, learning that two of the Witches' prophecies have
come true, is suddenly "rapt."[16] The term suggests demonic possession, especially since, as Wayne Shumaker records, "witchcraft, it is important to recognize, was everywhere and always
understood to involve a pact with the Devil."[17]

I fetch in the notion of demonic possession here not as the
"truth" about Macbeth's motivation—after all, ambition, "manliness," and uxoriousness are operative as well—but to emphasize
the extent to which Macbeth does not choose the murder but is
chosen by it, well before he stages it as an act in which he as well as
Duncan is victimized. Ravished on the heath by "horrible imaginings," he is unalterably committed to the deed. Later, in the
"If it were done" soliloquy, as the deed grows nearer, he has
moral misgivings, and voices them so eloquently that for a few
moments he dissuades himself. But these are the recriminations
and hesitations of a man on rails, of the lover who sees with perfect clarity every reason for abandoning a passion he cannot
abandon.[18]

Evil in Macbeth, then, is not a matter of being misguided. It is
not Plato's absence of a knowledge of the good, a simple case of
not knowing better. Macbeth *knows* to the deepest agenbite of
inwit. He comprehends a mortal ugliness that revolts and ob-
sesses him at the same time. But repellance, after all, is a measure
of desire. Anyone can long like Tamburlaine for the sweet fruition of an earthly crown. But to desire against the will is to give
desire its fullest due as an autonomous force. Macbeth knows
what it is he intends to do, and hates it, and does it anyway, and
makes us wonder with Eliot, "After such knowledge, what for-
giveness?" A question that answers itself.

Not that Shakespeare asks us to forgive Macbeth. He merely
asks us not to judge him too readily—not to dismiss him as
Aristotle's "thoroughly wicked man [who passes] from prosper-
ity to misfortune" (*Poetics*, 1453a), the kind of man whose fall will
elicit from the audience not a catharsis of pity and fear, whatever
that may mean, but unmitigated moral satisfaction. So he portrays Macbeth as a man who has "bought golden opinions from

all sorts of people," as one whose natural reluctance to do evil is testified to by his wife (disdainfully) and confirmed by his suffering before and after the deed, and yet as a man who nevertheless does evil not from ambition or calculation but from an inexplicable desire—a passion or infatuation beyond the reach of reason. In so doing Shakespeare rescues Macbeth from the category of melodramatic villain, the kind of character we can dismiss with a snap moral judgment, and elevates him to that of tragic hero, in whom good and ill are a mingled yarn and toward whom we must exercise a most careful moral and human discrimination if we are to do him even partial justice.

That, however, implies that we are Macbeth's judge. Perhaps so. As his epilogues repeatedly affirm, no one was more aware than Shakespeare that the audience's right to judge can be bought for a penny. And yet there is a sense in which Shakespeare denies us the full exercise of that right toward Macbeth. Let us return to the original question of why Shakespeare fails to dramatize the murder. To the partial answers we have already suggested we can add the theatrical necessity of shielding the tragic hero as criminal from the ill will of the audience. It is one thing for us to know that Macbeth murders Duncan, but it is quite another for us to see him at it. Hence Macbeth's horrible but invisible imaginings must not be allowed to materialize on stage as a horrifying deed. But for Shakespeare to omit the deed entirely would be to break faith with his audience, who have been promised a regicide. The deed must be absent, but it must also be present. How is this managed? By substituting for the unstaged deed a speech by Lady Macbeth that mediates between us and it, obscuring and revealing it at once. For although Lady Macbeth is before us on stage, her own horrible imaginings are in the bedchamber with her husband. If Duncan had not resembled her father, she says, she would have done the deed herself. Now, in a sense, she does do it.

And, alas, so do we.

For as we watch and listen to Lady Macbeth our imagination is in the bedchamber too, where the old and gracious Duncan lies sleeping, where the shriek of the owl cuts through the snores of the grooms as Macbeth pauses with the knives in his hands and then makes his way to the bed and . . . And what? Once, we know, he cries "Who's there?" perhaps having heard the grooms mutter "God bless us" and "Amen." Or was it a voice crying "Sleep no more! Macbeth does murder sleep"? And after that, how long does he stand looking down on the sleeping king before raising his knife? And as he plunges the knife into Duncan, does the old man's body surge upward in corporeal outrage? Do his hands clutch at Macbeth's? Do their eyes meet? Or does Duncan go gently into his deeper good night?

However we answer these questions, it is we who answer them and we who bear the guilt of our answers. Because it is we who imagine the deed into being, giving to "what is not" a local habitation and a name. Of course we are free *not* to imagine the deed—as free as Macbeth is not to perform it. That is, our freedom is as illusory as his, for of course he does perform it and we do imagine it. Indeed, he performs it *as* we imagine it. We are his accessories not before or after but, worse, during the fact. And if we cry mercy on the grounds that we could not help ourselves, given Lady Macbeth's suggestive remarks outside the chambers, we only bind ourselves more firmly to Macbeth. For his wife has seduced us both—him into doing the deed, us into imagining it.

"THE HORRID DEED"

Having indicted our guilty imaginations, let me somewhat perversely pursue the question of what we have imagined. "Perversely" because to discern in mere murder a metaphoric sexual act is bad enough. Still, having waded thus far into the sexual suggestiveness of Macbeth's deed of darkness, returning were at least as tedious as going o'er. What going o'er would take us through are the somewhat murky psychoanalytic depths of incest and parricide. Not that a parricidal explanation of Duncan's murder is unfamiliar. For instance Norman Rabkin makes the case, with appropriate qualifications, for a Macbeth who as it were "decides to kill Duncan out of the rage of a disappointed sibling"—disappointed, that is, because the nurturant Duncan has made Malcolm his heir.[19] The textual key to this view, Rabkin observes, is in Lady Macbeth's mysterious explanation for her own surprising inability to kill Duncan: "Had he not resembled / My father as he slept, I had done it," followed immediately by Macbeth's "I have done the deed."

Rabkin is dissatisfied, however, with the reductiveness of this explanation, concluding that "in the universe of Shakespearean tragedy, human behavior is governed by unknown and unknowable forces from within and without; it is no more reducible to the exclusive formulations of modern psychoanalysis than it is to those of seventeenth-century theology."

It would be hard to disagree. My own remarks about Macbeth's "falling in evil" as other men fall in love underscore the mysteriousness of Shakespearean motivation, in this respect so like motivation in actual life. For dramatists, after all, can assign motives with as much clarity as they like. But in *Macbeth,* and in Shakespeare generally, "categories," as Stephen Booth maintains, "will not define"; motives, meanings, concepts, and, as I have emphasized, even actions refuse to reside within the borders we assign them.[20] Thus the murder of Duncan becomes blurred as its literal identity of regicide shades off into sexual and now parricidal obscurities.

With parricide comes incest, to complete the Oedipal picture. If Duncan can assume the role of displaced father figure, then Lady Macbeth can assume the role of mother figure. To interpret it so, we would regard Macbeth's development in the play as an attempted graduation from child to man in which the crucial *rite de passage* is the murder of Duncan. To put it briefly: as child Macbeth wants immediate gratification of his desires. Thus we first hear of him in battle where the impulse to aggression finds immediate satisfaction in violence, which is not only its own reward but which inspires rewards from Duncan afterward. By the same token, Macbeth's desire to have the future now causes him to o'erleap the temporal obstacles to his predicted kingship and perform a present murder. And to this end he is governed by and dependent on his wife in the role of mother, who says "Leave all the rest to me" (1.5). It is she who will get him what he wants, who chides him like a child for not being a man, who would even murder Duncan for him had he not resembled her father, and who has to tidy up after him when he yields to childish fears: " 'Tis the eye of childhood / That fears a painted devil" (2.2.52).

The murder, then, whose sexuality we have already argued for, can now be seen as an act of incest and parricide in which Macbeth simultaneously kills the paternal Duncan and possesses the maternal Lady, thereby confirming his initiation from childhood into manliness.[21] But of course this is a brutal parody of a rite of passage to manhood, since in psychoanalytic theory the repression, not the commission, of the Oedipal act marks the most crucial stage in the child's maturation. Instead, Macbeth's deed represents the fulfillment of infantile desire and is hence an index of his failure to achieve authentic manhood. He fails even to achieve his wife's perverted concept of manhood, which consists in being, as the Second Apparition later puts it, "bloody, bold, and resolute." And so as he tries to assert his manhood further by murdering Banquo he employs agents—that is, he substitutes mediation and deferment for infantile immediacy—and at the same time takes the fledgling step of acting without his wife's maternal guidance, although it is still she whom he seeks to please and prove himself to: "Be innocent of the knowledge, chuck, till thou applaud'st the deed."

But that takes us beyond the deed in question. The point of Shakespeare's rendering regicide as a metaphoric act of incest and parricide—and that puts it too neatly (in the following chapter I shall try to ground this analysis in a fuller interpretation of the play)—is, I suppose, to endow it for us with the profoundly seductive repellance it has for Macbeth. At the same time, unlike Macbeth, we who have presumably repressed the impulse to this Oedipal act, who cannot o'erleap the tabus we have accepted, are brought back into contact with it, not immediately but through metaphoric and theatrical indirections, through an obscure hinting at motivations that lie too deep, as Rabkin suggests, for seventeenth-century thought. The fact that Shakespeare is portraying a "deed without a name" in the vocabulary of his culture—without a name until Freud named it—helps account for its (non)-performance offstage, in a darkness filled with intense but impenetrable suggestiveness. In what psychoanalysts call the return of the repressed, our imaginations touch the pitch of a primal scene, and recoil, as Macbeth does afterwards. Look on it again we dare not.

And so we are quick to deny our guilt: to know our deed, 'twere best not know ourselves. Better to reject Shakespeare's imagery. Or to argue, reasonably enough, that Macbeth's guilt is not our guilt. We have, after all, a perfect alibi: we were in our theater seats, not in Duncan's chambers. And if in a sense we were in Duncan's chambers, it was only imaginatively. Murders in the mind leave no indelible spots.

Yet we might do well to remind ourselves of the importance Shakespeare attaches to actions of the mind in *Macbeth*. He has taken extraordinary pains to show that the murder is not simply decided on but is conceived by outside suggestion and nurtured in the imagination, where it is likened to the raptness of demonic possession and from whence it issues into reality with something of the inevitability of an organic process. To imagine in *Macbeth* is not to depart from reality but to rehearse for it, the line between "If it were done" and "It is done" being most thin indeed. Without Macbeth's "thought, whose murder yet is but fantastical," without Lady Macbeth's imagined unsexings of herself, without Macbeth's hallucinated dagger and murderous fancies as he moves toward his design, and finally without our imaginative assistance, the deed could not be done.

"TO BE MORE THAN WHAT YOU WERE"

I noted earlier that as Macbeth moves with murderous intent toward Duncan's bedchamber, he makes an unlikely comparison of himself to Tarquin, a comparison that suggested an analysis of the murder as a metaphoric substitute for the sexual act—an uncreating deed of darkness. Let us now return to that comparison to suggest how its sexual import bears first on Macbeth's ambitious desire to augment his status and then on a kind of metadramatic formal desire in Shakespeare's play itself.

"Augment," in my last sentence, is an appropriate term because Shakespeare uses it in assessing Tarquin in *The Rape of*

Lucrece. His analysis of the self-destructiveness of desire in the following stanza is particularly relevant to Macbeth:

> So that in vent'ring ill we leave to be
> The things we are, for that which we expect;
> And this ambitious foul infirmity,
> In having much, torments us with defect
> Of that we have: so then we do neglect
>> The thing we have, and all for want of wit,
>> Make something nothing by augmenting it.
>>> (148–54)

Banquo makes use of this same word "augment" when he replies to Macbeth's vague suggestion that an alliance with him might gain Banquo future honor: "So I lose none / In seeking to augment it" (2.1.27). But even more relevant is Lady Macbeth's use not of the word but the idea when she urges her husband to augment his manhood:

> When you durst do it, then you were a man;
> And, to be more than what you were, you would
> Be so much more the man.   (1.7.51)

When Macbeth replies "I dare do all that may become a man; / Who dares do more is none," augmentation takes on the character of self-negating desire as it does in the stanza from *Lucrece*.

This making "something nothing by augmenting it" sounds rather like Jacques Derrida's concept of the "supplement"—that is, an excess added to a sufficiency, but paradoxically, because its presence implies a prior insufficiency, also a replacement of a lack.[22] Shakepeare's augmentation is even more extreme in that it not merely implies a lack in but effects a nullification of the prior state, making something nothing. On a large scale, that is the burden of the "My way of life" and "Tomorrow" speeches near the end of the play. Seeking to be more than what he was, Macbeth ultimately renders himself—and, in his despairing judgment, all of life—nothing.

As Shakespeare phrases it in the stanza from *Lucrece,* the problem of lust seems at first glance remediable since its cause is diagnosed as "want of wit." But the apparent remedy—to supplement wit—is merely a re-entry into the problem. Want of wit renders us conscious of a supposed want in "the thing we have." As a result "want" is transformed from a noun into a verb of desire, and the subsequent augmentive effort to satisfy desire reduces "all" to "nothing." We end up in a cybernetic loop that emblematizes the paradox of lust, to which Shakespeare also points ironically in the closing lines of Sonnet 129:

> All this the world well know; yet none knows well
> To shun the heaven that leads men to this hell.

These lines could be incorporated into *Lucrece* easily enough, but they could also refer to Macbeth in his "well knowing" but irresistible passion for the evil of murder, a murder the sonnet would characterize as "Past reason hunted and, no sooner had, / Past reason hated."

Let me trace this idea of augmentation in Macbeth's career, beginning back on the heath with the Witches' prophecies. Prophecy, as I suggested in the previous chapter, exaggerates certain features of ordinary speech; it writes wide the gap that exists in language between sign and presence, word and world. In a logocentric age the word substitutes for the world, representing it and at the same time deferring an engagement with it. In prophecy this deferral is explicitly announced and the future engagement scheduled, usually with judicious vagueness by the prophet—"the ides of March" for Caesar, merely "hereafter" for Macbeth. However, if the time of Macbeth's prophesied fulfillment is uncertain, the distance to be traveled is measured step by step, from Thane of Glamis to Thane of Cawdor to King of Scotland. The space between the first two of these is quickly covered by Ross's message from Duncan—"He bade me, from him, call thee Thane of Cawdor" (1.3.105). This augmentation of "Glamis" comes unexpectedly to Macbeth, who at this point feels no lack in his estate and anticipates no "additions"—"The Thane of Cawdor lives. Why do you dress me / In borrowed robes?" But once the addition is confirmed, the lack in his status is keenly felt.

For Macbeth the prophetic word is abstract and poor by comparison to the royal presence it promises, and the uncertainties of deferral are odious. Lady Macbeth may complain that he is too full of the milk of humankindness "to catch the nearest way," but that is not the Macbeth we see on the heath enraptured by thoughts of murder. Inspired by the Witches, he abruptly becomes a devotee of the pleasure principle and, like his wife, can no longer abide the detours of language and politics by which other men make their way in the world. As a violent subversion of natural due process, the murder will be an attempt to extort from time a premature presence, to augment "today" by ripping "tomorrow" untimely from its womb.

Before he commits a deed of prematurity, however, Macbeth experiences "horrible imaginings" that enable him to feel "the future in the instant." The gap between word and world, between prophetic promise and royal presence, is bridged by his imagination, which brings simulacra of presence before him so vividly that he is rapt. He does not elaborate on the Witches' promise of kingship by picturing crown, robe, and scepter but creates *ex nihilo* the "horrid image" of the murder by which he may achieve his royal ends. And yet we might argue that he is not imaginative enough. If he were, his imaginings would themselves prove satisfying substitutes for the murderous act. Compare Hamlet for instance. As mentioned earlier, when he stands over the praying Claudius his revenge is within sword's reach, yet he pauses, entertaining vivid images of a less likely future revenge, as though for him reality is less satisfying than the imaginings with which he supplements it. For Macbeth, however, the simulacra of presence, although intensely experienced, are merely the means to actual presence. Deeds must supplement the lack in thoughts. Thus the actual murder is like an experiment in evil, a hand-in-the-wound empirical act to determine how far beyond Macbeth's imaginings the reality may prove to be. His is a paradoxical case in which "something" (the seeming fullness of his life to this point) is made nothing by augmenting it, and at the same time in which "nothing" (his imaginings: "Nothing is but what is not") is made into a murderous something.

Shakespeare's word in *Macbeth* for what I have been calling "presence" seems to be "success," a term capable of meaning (according to the *OED*) "the prosperous achievement of something attempted, the attainment of an object according to one's desires"; "that which happens in the sequel, the termination of affairs, the result"; and "a succession as of heirs." That is, it may mean roughly a process (succession) or the conclusion of a process (with overtones of achievement). In its first appearance it refers to Macbeth's military achievement—"The King hath happily received, Macbeth, / The news of thy success" (1.3.89)—as it does when Macbeth writes to his wife about the Witches: "They met me in the day of success" (1.5.1). In this sense, the day is a satisfying time of achievement. And that is how Macbeth begins, in a state of presence, fulfillment, success—indeed, in the honors that come his way, almost an excess, as Lady Macbeth admits to Duncan when he thanks her for her hospitality:

> All our service
> In every point twice done, and then done double,
> Were poor and single business to contend
> Against those honours deep and broad wherewith
> Your Majesty loads our house.   (1.6.14)

Meanwhile, however, Macbeth has encountered the Witches and heard their prophecies, which he interprets as "supernatural soliciting," the seduction of the present by the promise of even greater success in the future: "Why [if it were ill] hath it given me earnest of success, / Commencing in a truth?" (1.3.132). Then later, in the famous soliloquy of 1.7, he says,

> If the assassination
> Could trammel up the consequence, and catch
> With his surcease success, that but this blow
> Might be the be-all and the end-all . . .

Success here means both process and achievement. Macbeth's hope is that the act that ends Duncan's life will also bring an end (surcease) to succession, of what might follow from the act. If so, the act will become a complete success by completing succession.

But as we have seen, the deed will not be done or complete and hence successful. The act that should end succession begins it instead, and therefore terminates success. Malcolm and Donalbain escape, and Banquo's issue stand to inherit the future. "To be thus," Macbeth says, "is nothing." And so this inadequate "being thus" must be augmented, by Banquo's death: "To be thus is nothing, / But to be safely thus" (3.1.47). One "thus" is to be made into a greater, more secure "thus." Although this second murder seeks to augment the first, filling a gap in the past, it also attempts to seize upon the future, capturing the royal success(ion) by terminating Banquo's "line." With the escape of Fleance, however, the augmentation proves equally incomplete, possessed of its own gap that needs filling ("Then comes my fit again. I had else been perfect"); and the succession that will lead ultimately to James I remains intact, receding always just beyond Macbeth's grasp.

The incompleteness of Macbeth's acts is correlative to the "want" of desire, which, as Sonnet 129 asserts, can never be satisfied. The transformation of "want" from noun to verb and back to noun is endless. The want in the title Thane of Glamis is supplemented by Macbeth's becoming Thane of Cawdor, which immediately becomes wanting by comparison to his being King of Scotland, which when achieved is wanting by comparison to Banquo's fathering a line of kings. So desire makes its insatiable way, each success "enjoyed no sooner but despised straight."

Macbeth's final act, the murder of Macduff's family, is meaningless. It follows upon his second meeting with the Witches. Frustrated by their hesitance to tell him whether Banquo's sons will be crowned, he demands an answer, "I will be satisfied" (4.1.104). And so he is. The deferral of presence that prophecy magnifies is erased, and Macbeth sees his worst fears realized as the Witches cry "Show! Show! Show!" and project a vision of Banquo's royal issue stretching out to the crack of doom. As Banquo's issue visually recede from Scotland and take royal form in England with James I, as even the Witches vanish, so news now arrives that Macduff has "fled to England." And Macbeth belatedly orders an assault on Macduff's castle, family, and heirs. Once he was before the fact; now he follows after.

The slaughter adds nothing to Macbeth's status; it has no bearing on the succession. Why then does he do it? In large part, for a very dull reason—from habit. Murder has become a reflex action for him. He does it, as Horatio explains the Gravemaker's ability to sing at his business, because "custom hath made it in him a property of easiness." A gravemaker himself, Macbeth has passed beyond "the initiate fear that wants hard use" (3.4.144) to the point where the fullness of success and presence comes not through the satisfaction of desire but through emotional and moral enervation: "I have supped full with horrors; / Direness . . . cannot once start me" (5.5.13). He no longer "wants" in either of that word's senses because he has completed his own dehumanization and grown sated with horrors.

"SO MUCH MORE THE MAN"

As a meaningless act of repetition, Macbeth's third murder forecasts the meaninglessness of his "Tomorrow" speech. What is meaningless about time in that speech is the failure of each successive day to add anything to its predecessors. The passage of time, like Macbeth's life, is merely a form of empty repetition whereby each day mirrors the others. Time is not more *than* what it was but only more *of* what it was. The distinction between "hereafter," when his wife would have died, and "now," when she does die, disappears along with the distinctions between each successive "tomorrow."

Perhaps one distinction at least can be coaxed from this speech. The tripling of the word "tomorrow" calls to mind the curious stress on triplicity and repetition that everyone notes in *Macbeth* but no one accounts for. Perhaps the most obvious reason for the triplings is to echo the triplicity of the Witches in the opening scene and thus to suggest the pervasiveness of demonic influence in Macbeth's world. But whatever reason we ascribe to them, in the present connection the effect of these triplings is to bring to the fore a difference between augmentation and "increase." Augmentation, as we have seen in *Lucrece* and Sonnet 129, is the mode of ambitious desire, figured paradigmatically in Shakespeare as lust, in which "want" shuttles from noun to verb and back again in endless pursuit of a heaven that on attainment becomes hell. The Witches' "I'll do, I'll do, and I'll do" gives triple emphasis to the futility of a lustful process that stretches out repetitively to the crack of doom. The verbal repetition suggests a plethora where in fact there is only emptiness, want, and insatiable desire. As with Macbeth's tomorrows, each successive act merely reproduces its predecessors and not only adds nothing to them but underscores their incompleteness.

For that matter, the three witches themselves present us with an appearance of fullness or abundance that is in fact mere redundancy. Three witches accomplish no more than one, either functionally (they act and speak alike) or visually (they look alike). They are simply one witch multiplied by three—an apparent variety that keeps returning to unity, as in their speech, which always verges on and frequently becomes chanting, all speaking as one while acting as one:

> Thus do go about, about
> Thrice to thine, and thrice to mine.
> And thrice again, to make up nine.   (1.3.34)

Which, we may wonder, is the first witch, the necessary one of whom the others are duplicates? No telling; they negate each other. The fullness of their repetitive presence dissolves as suddenly as they themselves.

Augmentation, then, can be associated with meaningless repetition, with making more of the same. Under this heading would fall Macbeth's three "done's" in his soliloquy, his three deeds of murder, the three mewings of the brinded cat, the triplicity of the Witches, their "I'll do, I'll do, and I'll do" and "Show! Show! Show!," the "Macbeth! Macbeth! Macbeth!" of the second apparition, and all similar verbal and actional forms of addition that follow, like Macbeth, the logic of becoming "more than what you were"—of becoming, as Anna Livia Plurabelle puts it, "mememormee."

But Shakespeare's term "augment" had another meaning as well, "increase." And if the former meaning is associated with lust, the latter is associated with procreation—which suggests that we shift our lyrical focus from Sonnet 129 to the first seventeen sonnets, in fact to the very first, which begins,

> Of fairest creatures we desire increase
> That thereby beauty's rose might never die.

From these early sonnets and the festive comedies, it becomes evident that children are a form of creative supplement. The young man of the sonnets is urged not to live as though he were an end unto himself, merely adding to his pleasure-trove like a miser, but to recognize that like all men he is wanting and in need of supplementation. His want is the inevitable consequence of his mortality and time's thievishness. Converting this want from a noun to a verb of sexual desire, which is Shakespeare's intent in this chastely pandering sonnet, does not result in an expense of spirit in a waste of shame, in mere lust, because what is spent is paradoxically saved, and what might be shameful is transcended by an act whose object is not selfish pleasure but the begetting of a child. Thus the young man will satisfy his mortal want by giving more of what he has, becoming immortal by living on in his line—not to mention his living on in the lines of these sonnets. He who is wanting gives, and in giving achieves increase. If in augmentation one loses by gaining, in procreation one gains by losing. Procreation, that is, is in both senses "yielding."

So Macbeth seeks to become more and becomes less. He is defeated by the forces of increase, by a world that, however ravaged by him, still possesses fullness and creative giving. At Inverness before the murder the "temple-haunting martlet" makes its "pendant bed and procreant cradle" everywhere: "Where they breed and haunt," Banquo says, "The air is delicate" (1.6). But Macbeth's deed of darkness, his metaphoric act of lust, converts this "temple" into the Porter's hell, as the promiscuity of Sonnet 129 transforms a desired heaven into an achieved hell. On the other hand, when Banquo hears the prophecies, he does not seek to augment his present state with a fuller presence. Because he has re-presented himself in his son, however, he fathers ultimately a line of kings (and queens) that stretches, if not to the crack of doom, at least into the eighteenth century. Duncan has re-presented himself in Malcolm, Banquo in Fleance, Macduff in his son, even old Siward in his son. By contrast, the mysterious absence of Macbeth's children stresses the sterility of his self-love. Instead of creating himself anew, he simply swells to monstrous proportions. Having much, yet tormented with defect of what he has, he strives beyond the present toward illusions of a plethoric future, and so like Tarquin "makes something nothing by augmenting it."

"IT IS DONE"

Let me turn now from Macbeth's deeds to Shakespeare's deed, in hopes that the plight of the hero can tell us something about the plight of the playwright. Perhaps a good place to begin is with the "Tomorrow" speech, in which Macbeth calls on theatrical imagery to record his response to the news of his wife's death. Life as he now sees it is no more than the brief strutting and fretting of a poor player before he falls silent and is heard no more, and the sum of all our yesterdays is an idiot's tale signifying nothing. Considered metadramatically, the interest of this speech lies not in the light shed by theater on life and time but just the reverse. Taking a broader view than Macbeth, we can see that "poor" players are not alone in suffering quick extinction. Time will have its way with good ones too, and indeed with all playing and plays to boot. It is in the nature of theater that what is performed on stage is as mortal as Lady Macbeth, who died not "hereafter" but now. This mortality is demonstrated most graphically when the curtain falls, but no less significantly moment by performed moment as the play creeps or more likely hastens to its daily demise. In the irreversible flow of enactment each phase of the play—each scene, speech, even word—is no sooner manifest than it disappears and is heard no more—a far cry from the indelibility Shakespeare ascribes to his printed sonnets: "Not marble nor the gilded monuments / Of princes shall outlive this powerful rhyme" (Sonnet 55). Moreover, given this remorseless disappearance of the play into its own grave as it moves toward silence, *Macbeth* is as much threatened by meaninglessness as the life its hero speaks of. Surely that possibility is implicit in the speech itself. How, then, is this empty succession of time transcended? How does the experience of *Macbeth* escape the experience of Macbeth?

We should first observe that this quick mortality of the dramatic mode—its being done-with as soon as it is done—is hardly peculiar to *Macbeth*. In *Hamlet* for instance the same notion is summed up in the ambiguity of the word "consummation." As though reflecting the suicidal longings of its princely hero, the play *Hamlet* consumes itself in the process of being consummated—its substantial theatrical images melting, thawing, and resolving themselves into a dew, the seemingly substantial words of its characters evaporating breathily into empty air as soon as they are spoken. To resist this impulse to theatricide Shakespeare makes the most of delay—not merely by advertising Hamlet's procrastination but by calling on a vast dramaturgical repertoire of interrupting, arresting, and deferring tactics. [23]

To take this a bit further, in *Hamlet* the hero's task is to bring the lost past into the present, modeling himself on the Ghost, itself a disembodiment of the past that emerges in the present with the words "Remember me!" But Hamlet defers his task, in effect forgetting the Ghost in favor of exploring himself and his world—in short, by living despairingly in the present alone, in a cleft between past and future. *Hamlet* itself does much the same by magnifying the present moment in the ways I have indicated. Ultimately, with the act of revenge, Hamlet remembers the ghostly past and retrieves from it an otherwise forgotten and unknown murder. Then the play ends with the trustee of the future, Fortinbras, kept waiting, his kingship deferred while he listens to Horatio telling Hamlet's story. With this story *Hamlet* will metamorphose from transient drama into memorializing narrative, as if the play were answering its own ghostly appeal to "Remember me!"

Now this, I suggest, is very nearly the reverse of what happens in *Macbeth*, where the witchy equivalents of the Ghost cry not "Remember me!" but "Foresee thyself!" Their prophecies both imply a model to follow and constitute a temptation not to do so. On the one hand, that is, they imply that deferral is the unavoidable human mode, that the present is inevitably deficient. Yet on the other hand, precisely because the present is deficient and the future full of promise, the prophecies tempt Macbeth to demand that the future be now. To bring the future into the present Macbeth must act, appropriately enough because action is future-oriented. But action is future-oriented not merely in being pur-posive but also in being, as we have seen, unending. It takes place now but it issues into the future instead of disappearing securely into the past, as Macbeth would wish. Thus it is dangerously undone. Realizing this, Macbeth takes arms against the future—against Banquo's line and Macduff's heirs. But the future takes its revenge with the army of Malcolm and Macduff, and in the suc-cession of kings fathered by Banquo. Toward the end, what should have been "hereafter" becomes "now" as Lady Macbeth commits suicide, and the endless tomorrows stretching out be-fore Macbeth are somehow already "recorded" to the last syllable and hence are impregnable to his desire.

If prophecy undoes Macbeth in this fashion, what about the audience? For of course we too hear the Witches' prophecies, which are Shakespeare's means of conveying to us his own dra-matic prophecies. The words that cause Macbeth to foresee a murder and a crowning in Scotland cause us to foresee a murder and a crowning in the theater. As a result, ambitious desire on the heath takes the form of dramatic expectation in the Globe.

It would seem, then, that our experience parallels Macbeth's.[24] However, there is a significant difference. As we saw in the pre-vious section, Macbeth's augmentive mode of desire seeks to sub-vert the deferral of presence to which desire is inevitably subject. But this only inaugurates a series of uncompleted acts that de-generate into meaningless repetition. In the end desire is not satisfied for Macbeth but suffocated by excess, and the future be-longs to those who like Duncan and Banquo are fulfilled not so much in themselves as in their increase, in the lineal succession that passes with Fleance out of the play itself and into a long-deferred future that is a fulfilled present for James I and his play-wright subject.

This succession-as-increase may be said to characterize the movement of the play itself. It is a procreative process wherein an apparent fullness is seen to be wanting and in need of supplemen-tation. This has the appearance of Macbeth's desire to become more than what he is, but whereas Macbeth's desire "makes something nothing by augmenting it," the play makes something into a greater something by fulfillment. Just as "success" is paradoxically an ongoing process and an achieved conclusion, so the play is both a continuous linear performance in time and a series of dramatic accomplishments. Viewed only as a continuous experience, the play tends to sacrifice its present to its future, just as prophecy casts our imaginations, with Macbeth's, beyond the immediate moment toward the fulfilling future. Thus as we noted earlier, the opening scene of the play is in a sense effaced by the Witches' prophecy of a future meeting with Macbeth, and Macbeth's present experience on the heath is effaced by his rapt imaginings of the future murder.

On the other hand, as a series of dramatic accomplishments, the play transcends its own transiency by making each phase of its succession a success. What is for Macbeth an obliviousness to the present brought on by his rapt absorption in future possibilities is for the audience a marvelous theatrical moment full of eloquence, tension, and intrinsic fascination. What is for him horrible imaginings is for us an electrifying speech about horrible imaginings. By the same token, the opening scene with the Witches, seemingly modest and self-effacing, is rendered theatrically arresting by virtue of its incantatory verse and the visual interest of the Witches themselves. Thus the arousal of expectation in the audience does not necessarily erase the present theatrical moment, as it might if suspense were Shakespeare's only goal. The aesthetic effect of Shakespeare's deferrals is not to impoverish but to enrich the present. By charting the theatrical future, his prophetic form secures its uncertainties and enables us to attend more fully to the present—to a present which we perceive not in isolation but within the context of evolving destiny.

Thus if the prophecies arouse in Macbeth an impulse to rip the future untimely from its womb, they create in us a reassuring sense of dramatic form and meaning. The illusion of destiny imparted by the Witches' prophecies implies a governing unity in human affairs—a world whose apparently random evolution in time is at a deeper level a kind of form in suspense. This describes the action of the play also. The dramatic mode may be a succession of present tense experiences suggestive of Macbeth's "tomorrow and tomorrow and tomorrow," but by means of prophecy Shakespeare advertises a destiny at work in the theater that imparts order to the transient and meaning to the pointless. The Witches are, as Macbeth says, "imperfect speakers" not only because they do not reveal everything, but also because only the future can perfect their foretellings. As mentioned earlier, Macbeth's accession to the throne, the movement of Birnam Wood to Dunsinane, the killing of Macbeth by one not of woman born: such events are fully meaningful only when regarded as "that which was foretold." So it is with all events in the play, which either grow out of the dramatic past or plant the seeds of the future.[25] If the movement of Birnam Wood to Dunsinane is forecast in the Witches' prophecies, the murder of Duncan is embryonic in Macbeth's proleptic imaginings, even in his new-won title Thane of Cawdor, which identifies him as a treasonous rebel. From Lady Macbeth's "A little water clears us of this deed" in Act 2 issues her ritualistic handwashing in Act 5, and from Macbeth's fixing of McDonwald's head on the battlements in Act 1 comes Macduff's entrance in Act 5 with Macbeth's own head on his pike. Such occurrences fulfill the formal promises implicit in Shakespeare's plot and by satisfying expectations in the audience give shape to theatrical time.

The play proceeds, then, less by augmentation than by increase, by a procreativity that contrasts with the barrenness of Macbeth's reign. The dramatic future is planted prophetically in the present and brought to fruition and harvest in good season. The announcement of a want in the present generates a wanting in both Macbeth and us, and at the same time assures us that this lack/desire will be filled/satisfied in the future. For us, if not for Macbeth, that is repeatedly the case. The subsequent actions of the play perfect Shakespeare's theatrical prophecies much as a son in his sonnets and comedies retroactively perfects his father's lack of and desire for immortality. Yet in another sense the process is endless. Each fulfillment creates a lack to be filled. Even the death of the tyrant and the triumphant entrance of Malcolm are a promised end and at the same time an unending, a freeing of the time for regeneration, for all that would be "newly-planted." This apparent fullness of final presence—the apparent closure of an end—fades even as it appears, and we are asked to think of the play, just beyond its formal end, not as gathering up its past narratively, as Horatio is to do in *Hamlet,* but as forecasting its future dramatically. Malcolm invites everyone not to hear a story about Macbeth and the past but to "see" his own crowning at Scone. If this sense of an unending suggests a want in *Macbeth,* however, it is a want that can be satisfied only by *Macbeth* itself, each representation of which will reveal a further want that, as we all can testify, will only make the play the more wanted.

Three

Macbeth: Violence

and Meaning

FRIEND OF mine once watched a television showing of *Macbeth* with an elderly American Indian woman, who afterwards sat silent for a while, then shook her head and said, "What barbarians you white people are!" With her background surely she did not need *Macbeth* to tell her that. But perhaps she was surprised to discover that the white man actually publicizes his barbarity, staging it in theaters and on television as a cultural achievement. Still, better *Macbeth* than Wounded Knee. Not that *Macbeth* is more sadistic than *Titus Andronicus* or more violent than *Henry VI, Richard III,* or *Coriolanus*. But it may be more archaically savage than they. When Banquo's ghost appears at the feast in Act 3 the dismayed Macbeth says "Blood has been shed ere now, in the olden time, / Ere humane statute purged the gentle weal" (3.4.76). However, this statutory gentling of violence is rendered somewhat suspect when Macbeth adds "Ay, and since too, murders have been performed / Too terrible for the ear." Certainly his own bloody career demonstrates that "olden time" is not so distant. Indeed the Scotland of this play seems almost Hobbesian, a place of whinstone and barren heaths where life, beginning with a battle and ending with a battle, is nasty, brutish, and decidedly short. It is as though Shakespeare had decided to dramatize Albany's remark in *King Lear* about humanity preying on itself like monsters of the deep (4.2.50).

This barbarity is usually attributed to Macbeth. Into an ordered society governed by a benevolent monarch he introduces radical and bloody disorder, transforming not merely his own castle, where "heaven's breath smells wooingly," but all of Scotland into a hell that beggars the Porter's drunken imaginings. Then gradually the essential goodness of man and nature reasserts itself under the quasi-divine sanction of an English king. The tyrant is destroyed, the time is declared free, a new king is about to be anointed. In the national long run Macbeth's rule is a tyrannic interlude between the gracious reigns of Duncan and his rightful successor Malcolm, a fearsome reminder of the brutal abnormalities that befall man or nation when evil is unleashed.

This is a familiar, coherent, and surely for the most part persuasive way of looking at *Macbeth*. Still, it may leave us with some small dissatisfactions. There is, for instance, the perennial question about the mysterious birth of evil out of good. If nature and culture in Scotland are governed by God and founded on order, harmony, and moral purpose, what gives rise to disorder, violence, and evil, especially in a man as favored as Macbeth? Why should a nobleman of wealth and power, a military hero recently dignified by his king, a man of conscience and humankindness, abruptly abandon the values he has lived by and murder the King who sustains him in particular and his society in general? Most of the answers to these questions, however varied in their details, proceed from a kind of Manichean assumption that Macbeth's evil can be sharply divided from the prevailing Scots good. This assumption is not so much wrong, I think, as in need of some supplementary shading to account for the fact that savagery is so deeply ingrained in Scots culture.[1] I propose, therefore, to take a kind of psycho-sociological look at the play to observe the role played by violence and culture in the formation and deformation of Macbeth's self.[2]

Homo homini lupus

When men do violence to one another, especially if it is vicious or sadistic, they usually assault language as well by labeling their behavior brutal or bestial. Shakespeare and Macbeth are no exception. Thus when Lady Macbeth prods her husband to keep his murderous promise to her, he hesitates, fearing that if he dares do more than may become a man he will become "none," a beast. Perhaps the beast he has in mind is the wolf, since he later assigns a wolf to accompany him and "withered murder" on their way to Duncan's chambers, and since for Shakespeare the wolf habitually emblematizes the ravenings of inhuman appetite. But of course the trouble with Shakespeare's zoology is that man is more inhuman than wolves, or, alas, more human. Thus if the bestialized Macbeth were likened to a wolf it would have to be a wolf lacking the inhibitive mechanism that prevents it from killing its own kind. As Konrad Lorenz has shown, such biological mechanisms have evolved among highly aggressive and potentially lethal family animals to preserve the species; and since man possesses the lethal capacity in abundance but lacks instinctive inhibitions he is the most self-destructive of animals.[3]

There is no news here. The self-destructive animal has taken ample note of its own viciousness and has even drawn a wolfish conclusion in an expression common in Shakespeare's time, *homo homini lupus.* "Man is a wolf to man" because biology works better than culture. In Shakespeare's *homo Scotus,* for instance, the inhibitions of wolfish instinct take symbolic form as the Judeo-Christian "Thou shalt not kill," to which are added in Macbeth's case the constraints implicit in his being Duncan's kin, his host, and his subject. Unfortunately cultural tabus are less reliable than wolfish inhibitions. Lorenz reports that when the losing wolf in a fight displays the appropriate submissive gesture, exposing its throat to the victor, the latter continues to snarl and bristle and even feint at its helpless opponent—that is, it gives every indication of still wanting to kill, yet it cannot.[4]

In *Macbeth* the situation is similar up to a point. Like the vulnerable wolf making its gesture of submission, the trusting Duncan exposes his throat to Macbeth's mercy. He enters the castle, eats his food, even falls asleep, albeit with guards outside. But Macbeth is almost precisely the reverse of the dominant wolf. In his "If it were done" speech and afterwards, he gives every indication of wanting to preserve Duncan's life, but he simply cannot, especially when his wife reinforces his savage desire.

Does this imply that Macbeth is motivated by a murderous nature, by an evil so nearly instinctive as to override all cultural inhibitions? Surely there is some truth in that. But as Bernard Spivack has argued, Macbeth is not Aaron the Moor, or Richard Crookback, or Iago.[5] Lacking the "milk of humankindness" Macbeth is supposed to possess, these characters are villains proper. Bestial and wolfish, in Shakespeare's sense, they were born with teeth and a psychopathic indifference to moral norms. Hence they are the stuff of modern science fiction, malevolent aliens who merely look human. As a result they constitute a far less disturbing presence than Macbeth, who is not alien but one of us and yet somehow not one of us. In fact he is too much one of us—a man honored for his manhood yet who nevertheless wants to be "so much more the man."

Still there is some truth in the idea that Macbeth has a murderous nature. After all, like Coriolanus he is a warrior, a professional "unseamer" of men's bodies. Violence is part of what Renaissance humanists would call his "special" nature, an individual addition to his general "humankindness," and in Scotland it is an excellent thing in a man, at least on the battlefield where "Thou shalt not kill" has no force. "Thou shalt kill" guides Macbeth, and in pursuing this principle he is wolfish indeed—disemboweling and dismembering his enemies, making "strange images of death," even seeming about to bathe in reeking wounds. He does everything wolfish except devour his victims. And in a sense he wants to do that as well. Not for the calories—for the meaning. He wants to conquer and grow large by swallowing what is far more energy-giving than his enemy's flesh—his distinctively human significance.

This grows a bit ghoulish. Let me try to find some textual justification for this metaphor of semantic cannibalism by suggesting that if we were to interpret *Macbeth* by keying on its most famous lines we would regard the "Tomorrow" speech as a thematic terminus toward which the hero's experience has been working. Macbeth's remarks about the death of meaning—a world "full of sound and fury, signifying nothing"—presuppose a former life of meaning. In fact, if life is a walking shadow because its path leads to dusty death, as it just has for Lady Macbeth, then it is death that destroys meaning. Not just the death of Lady Macbeth, though that hits close to home, and not death in general. Macbeth has seen enough men go down in battle to know that "all our yesterdays" are candling us into darkness. But those are outside facts. At this point in the play, however, within or beyond the generalizations and personifications of the famous moving lines, lies Macbeth's visceral awareness of death as the most personal and intimate of certainties. Not the knowledge that "man" dies, but that "Macbeth" will die. For "man" never dies; he lives forever in his abstract Platonic haven. Only creatures of flesh and bone like Macbeth die.

This most unwolflike awareness comes hard to all of us, but especially to a man assured by truth-telling witches that he bears "a charmed life" and cannot be killed by a man born of woman. If the Witches' prophecy seems to Macbeth a guarantee of immortality, at least as far as violent death is concerned, then Shakespeare seems to be pairing off immortality and meaning against death and meaninglessness. Looking back over the play we would expect to find the former leading to the latter. If we look back far enough, however, we come to a violent beginning which is as full of death and meaninglessness as Macbeth's "Tomorrow" speech.

THE MATRIX OF MEANING

Violence, according to Heraclitus, is a constructive force. "War is father of all, king of all, and he shows some to be gods and some to be men: he makes some slaves and some free" (Frag. 44). The seeds of an interpretation of *Macbeth* might lie in this, if we could discern which grain will grow and which will not. Let us at any rate attempt to witch a few meanings from the play by adopting a Heraclitean perspective, beginning at the beginning, which, I argued earlier, is not a beginning at all.

If we ask why Shakespeare begins with the Witches, surely a piece of an answer is that he wants to extend the play's range of reality into mysterious regions and to suggest an evil, perhaps diabolical dimension to its events. In several respects the Witches are marginal entities. Theatrically they constitute the threshold of the play. Encountering them the audience crosses from the realities of the Globe to the illusions of Scotland. At the same time, within Scotland, they exist at the border between the realities of the battlefield and the unrealities of the otherworld. And finally they hover at the border of the second scene. Thus as they depart from one side of the stage and Duncan's group enters from the other, suddenly in the place where we last saw them there appears the figure of the bloody Captain, and we may wonder if the Witches have completely gone. For an instant the bloody image of violence is framed against the mysterious and otherworldly. And the fact that throughout this scene we may hear but never see the fighting reinforces this impression that violence takes place in its own dark domain.

This slight blurring of distinctions suggests that the "hurly-burly" of the battle scenes is Scotland's version of what René Girard calls the "sacrificial crisis"—when violence destroys the social and individual distinctions that define an ordered community.[6] Information theorists tell us that when entropy prevails, messages are drowned by noise—that is, meaningful distinctions are lost in general undifferentiation. We could say, then, that *Macbeth* begins with noise, with the undifferentiations of the three Witches, who look alike, speak alike, and act alike, whose ambiguous appearance blurs the distinctions between male and female and between "inhabitants of the earth" and "not of the earth" (1.3.41), and whose oracular pronouncements confuse fair and foul and lost and won. It is conventional of course that sybils, witches, and demons should mask their messages in the noise of ambiguity, paradox, and riddle. Since such clashing sounds and meanings are a kind of verbal violence, the Witches strike a properly cacophonous keynote to the battle scene that follows, indeed to the play that follows.

Undifferentiation takes visual as well as auditory forms. The battle scene opens with Duncan's question "What bloody man is that?" Blood here is the visual noise that masks the "message" of identity. For blood is indistinguishably common. In the absence of a hematologist, all men are alike inside the veins. Thus the entrance of a momentarily unidentifiable "bloody man" proclaims the fact that battlefield violence masks individuality, reducing everyone to the status of reflex killing and desperate survival. Significantly, then, the Captain reports that the warring armies are indistinguishable—like "two spent swimmers, that do cling together" (1.2.10). In this strange analogy the warriors are less combatants than victims, not so much fighting one another as attempting to survive in the tides of shed blood surging around them. More specifically in this vein, the Captain labels McDonwald "merciless"—by comparison, we should expect, to a more charitable Macbeth—yet adds that it is Macbeth who, forgoing such civilities as handshakes and farewells, viciously unseams the rebel from "the nave to the chops" (24). And again later on Macbeth is indistinguishable from the Thane of Cawdor when he confronts him "with self-comparisons, / Point against point" and, in a curiously undiscriminating adjective, "rebellious arm against arm" (58). So indistinguishable are they, in fact, that later, by grace of Duncan's entitlement, Macbeth becomes "Thane of Cawdor."

Rebels, royalists, Norwegians, kerns, gallowglasses: all are bloodily one in battle—bloody in heart and in mind. Blood is a mortal reminder.[7] To be capable of bleeding is to be capable of dying. Yet to spill the blood of men who would spill yours is, apart from eating, the most rudimentary form of self-preservation. Thus from the undifferentiating violence of battle, where men are like so many beasts striving to escape death by inflicting it, the victor rises with special distinction. He is alive. That, for any creature, is the primal difference, the fundamental meaning. And what more convincing way to demonstrate this violently earned meaning than to sever your enemy's head from his trunk, as Macbeth does McDonwald's, and fix it high on the battlements? For the wisdom of the turtle reminds us that from a creaturely point of view the head, whatever else it may be, is also the most vital and vulnerable appendage of the body.

In the human anatomical tragedy, the head is the source of hubris. Put plainly, it sticks out—both to individualize and to endanger us.[8] Or, to be more accurate, it sticks *up,* and in doing so it distinguishes man from beast, according to Elizabethan moralists, who did not know that the tragedy of *Tyrannosaurus Rex* preceded that of *Oedipus Rex.* Man's first presumption—this raising of his head to become more than a beast—is perpetuated in his efforts to elevate his head above those of his fellow men. As a rebel, McDonwald himself has sought to thrust himself up out of the undifferentiated mass of mere subjects and proclaim his difference by challenging the King. And on the bloody battlefield he and Macbeth are alike in trying to keep their heads above an undifferentiating flood of violence. But this likeness between them is as short-lived as McDonwald himself. When the battle is over, the fundamental difference is plain to every man's eye: Macbeth's head is on his neck, McDonwald's ornaments a pole.

Macbeth survives, McDonwald does not. Survival is more than a matter of staying alive. "The moment of *survival,*" Elias Canetti writes, "is the moment of power."[9] Or in Heraclitus's phrase, war makes some to be gods and some to be men. His use of the term "gods" may be not simply a loose hyperbole but an acknowledgment that a man who survives death in battle has some claim to being more than a man, becoming, if only for the moment, like the gods—immortal. As Otto Rank wrote, "the death fear of the ego is lessened by the killing, the sacrifice, of the other; through the death of the other, one buys oneself free from the penalty of dying, of being killed."[10] Thus the battlefield is Macbeth's proving ground, where he puts his mortality to the test. Like most warriors he fights not merely for his own life or for king and country but to distinguish and justify himself, to "immortalize" himself, in the sense of achieving life not after death but before it, of acquiring power over death and hence an illusion of deathlessness.[11] It is especially fitting, then, for the Captain to report Macbeth's status by saying that when he proceeded against Cawdor he did so as "Bellona's bridegroom, lapped in proof" (1.2.57). To be wedded to the goddess of war, herself immortal, is to acquire immortality oneself, to be "proof" against death. For those whom war makes mere men the presence of death is merely a reminder of their own vulnerable mortality. For heroes like Macbeth it is a confirmation of specialness. He does not fear death because in the intoxication of battle he *is* death. Thus when Ross tells him with an air of wonder that in battle he was "nothing afeard of what thyself didst make, / Strange images of death" (1.3.96), his phrasing is sufficiently ambiguous to suggest that Macbeth not only killed other men but assumed the aspect of death as he did so.

As Shakespeare portrays him, then, Macbeth is less a general, a field tactician like Henry V, than a killer, a battlefield survivor who takes definition from the deaths of others. That he achieves his identity by transcending death is made explicit when the Witches prophesy that he will graduate from Glamis to Cawdor to king. "By Sinel's death," he says, "I know I am Thane of Glamis, / But how of Cawdor? The Thane of Cawdor lives." By virtue of surviving his father he became Thane of Glamis, and now by virtue of surviving his enemy he becomes Thane of Cawdor. Taking the titles of those who die, he feeds off death, like the primitive warrior who absorbs the power of his slain enemy by eating his flesh and assuming his name.[12] So death defines Macbeth and enlarges him. He stands over dead men on the battlefield, he is singled out by the Witches immediately afterward for prophetic glory, he is honored by the King with a thaneship. And all for killing. Why should he doubt that death will make him King of Scotland?

SACRED VIOLENCE

The battlefield is a scene of undifferentiated brutality yet a place where significant differences are made known, where some are shown to be gods and some to be men. However, there is another difference that forces itself upon our attention from the very beginning of the battle scene—the spatial difference that marks

Duncan off from the battle. For unlike most of Shakespeare's kings, Duncan is not on the field with his men but standing in the foreground receiving information about the warriors fighting offstage. *He* is eminently and distinctively here; *they* are an invisible mass of violence there, represented by clanging metal, wild cries, alarums—a gross amplification of the messageless noise of the Witches' opening speeches—and by the bloodiness of the Captain who comes to report. This spatial distance between king and warriors reflects the sociopolitical difference between king and subjects and suggests that the violence somehow takes its origin in this difference.

For we can hardly help noting how completely unmotivated the fighting in this scene is. Shakespeare almost perversely refuses to tell us why McDonwald and Cawdor rebel and Sweno invades. In Holinshed the reason for the rebellion is clear enough: McDonwald regards Duncan as a kind of Henry VI, a "faint-hearted milksop more meet to govern a sort of idle monks in some cloister than to have the rule of such valiant and hardy men of war as the Scots were." Cawdor has no part in the rebellion, and the Norwegians under Sweno invade, as Norwegians periodically will, hoping "to subdue the whole realm of Scotland."[13] In Shakespeare's treatment, however, McDonwald is "worthy to be a rebel" for the unenlightening reason that "multiplying villainies of nature / Do swarm upon him" (1.2.12); and Cawdor, who according to Angus (1.3.111) may have combined with the Norwegians or may have aided the Scots rebels ("[which] I know not"), later confesses his "treasons," but what his treasons are or why he committed them we never learn. Nor do we learn anything about Sweno. The three men are simply labeled rebels and traitors, as though their significance lies exclusively in their rising, for whatever reason, against the King. Thus we witness (via narrative) a battle from which all we can infer is that one side fights against the King and the other for him. The impression given is that violence arises not from anything Duncan himself has done but from the mere fact of kingship itself, the royal difference.[14]

By leaving us without an explicit reason for the battle Shakespeare strips violence of its rational pretenses and obliges us to confront it as a stark primitive fact, a kind of primal given, like

Chaos, the nothingness from which God fashioned Creation. At this level the King acquires a special status. His being on high ground, safely above the maelstrom in which lesser men drown, suggests that although he may be the ultimate target of violence, still death cannot reach him. Not yet, at any rate. What was said earlier about Macbeth earning a form of deathlessness by surviving the battle applies even more forcefully to Duncan. The mere fact that the battle is taking place testifies to his greatness: men die so the King may live. The Captain has even risked his life so the King's son may live. If the battle is a test for the warrior Macbeth it is all the more so for King Duncan. It is an ordeal by combat. As Johan Huizinga pointed out, war is a form of divination.[15] It enables kings to look into the entrails of violence and see if they are still sacred to the gods.

Let me cite an archaic parallel. Sir James Frazer's *The Golden Bough* gets its title from the story of the King of the Wood, the name given the priest who guarded the forest sanctuary of Diana beside a lake near the modern town of Nemi. The King of the Wood was a murderer, having obtained his royal status by stalking and killing his predecessor, as he in his turn would be stalked and killed by his successor. While he was in office the priest-king personified the spirit of the oak tree on which grew the "golden bough"—the mistletoe in which the life of the priest-king and of the god-spirit within the tree was thought to reside. As long as the mistletoe remained on the tree the King of the Wood was invulnerable, but if it were seized and hurled at him—especially, one supposes, along with a knife—he died. As might be expected, the King of the Wood spent much of his sleepless reign guarding the tree.[16]

Frazer is not much concerned with the priest-king's motive for aspiring to this hazardous office. He apparently assumes that the honor of serving Diana and the god within the tree was its own reward. Perhaps so, but this honor was so bound up with potential death as to suggest a supplementary motive: the would-be King of the Wood may have answered the sylvan call not despite its hazards but because of them, because in his kingly role the constantly impending presence of death endowed his life with transcendent meaning and being. Each day, each moment even, was a triumphant evasion of violent death, a renewal of one's sacred immunity. This is especially so inasmuch as the King of the Wood is defended by the god he defends. Even when the king is killed, however, the god does not die; he merely takes up residence in the new king. Indeed kings are killed *because* the god leaves them. Then they are merely men and mortal. Thus each fight with a challenger who would kill him is a test of the king's sacredness: will the golden bough remain on its branch? will the god's strange heart still beat within his own?

Holinshed's historical Duncan shared the plight of the King of the Wood.[17] He was simply one of a series of eleventh-century Scottish kings who were slain by their successors. But as Shakespeare has dramatized it, Duncan is more than merely a tribal chieftain with a crown up for grabs; he is a secular divinity of sorts, different not merely in "degree" but almost in kind from other men. None of the tragedies calls on this conception of kingship so insistently as *Macbeth,* which in this respect is a throwback to history plays like *Richard II,* but which is probably also a reflection of King James's Divine Right views of monarchy. As God's vicar, the anointed king has the gift, the touch, the power, or, in a word that kindles the imaginations of Lord and Lady Macbeth, "greatness." In his sacredness he must not be approached too closely without averting the eyes and unhinging the knees. Like the sun he sustains nature and men, radiating warmth, life, and fertility, as when Duncan tells Macbeth,

> I have begun to plant thee, and will labor
> To make thee full of growing. Noble Banquo,
> That hast no less deserved, nor must be known
> No less to have done so, let me infold thee
> And hold thee to my heart.

BANQUO: There if I grow,
> The harvest is your own.

DUNCAN: My plenteous joys,
> Wanton in fullness, seek to hide themselves
> In drops of sorrow. —Sons, kinsmen, thanes,
> And you whose places are the nearest, know
> We will establish our estate upon

> Our eldest, Malcolm, whom we name hereafter
> The Prince of Cumberland; which honor must
> Not unaccompanied invest him only,
> But signs of nobleness, like stars, shall shine
> On all deservers.

When such a king dies—when, as MacDuff says, "sacrilegious murder hath broke ope / The Lord's anointed temple and stole thence / The life of the building"—then the sun dies, the crops wither, winter comes, animals violate their natural bonds, order collapses.

Savage as it is, then, battle is nevertheless a sacred activity, a ceremony of violence in which warriors like Macbeth and Banquo play the role of priests sacrificing bodies to the god-king. This view of violence takes its toll on conventional values. The Captain's report contains several examples of a kind of moral schizophrenia that seems to afflict the Scots. There is, for instance, his statement that Macbeth, once he had carved his way to McDonwald,

> never shook hands, nor bade farewell to him,
> Till he unseamed him from the nave to the chops,
> And fixed his head upon our battlements.

Did the Captain really expect Macbeth to shake hands with McDonwald and bid him farewell as a prelude to gutting him? In recoil from this we search for irony, only to encounter Duncan's approving response: "O valiant cousin, worthy gentleman!" We are left with a grotesque juxtaposition of manners and massacre that can be accounted for, evidently, only if we assume that in the holy cause of violence the unseaming of a rebel *is* the act of a "worthy gentleman," for the rebel is a heretic, not fully human.

That this is not simply a lapse of tone is evidenced by a highly similar occasion later in the scene—when the Captain attempts to explain the fury of Banquo and Macbeth's counterattack on the Norwegians by suggesting that perhaps they intended "to bathe in reeking wounds, / Or memorize another Golgotha" (1.241). He seems to say that he regarded them as warriors so intoxicated by bloodlust as to be capable of reenacting the Crucifixion. Again a search for signs of irony is brought up short by Duncan's response: "So well thy words become thee as thy wounds; / They smack of honor both." Instead of irony, then, we apparently encounter a devotion to violence so fanatic that neither the Captain nor the King even registers this grotesque collusion of bloodthirstiness and Christian imagery. Instead the imagery seems intended to sanctify the bloodshed. As priestly leaders of the royal forces Macbeth and Banquo preside over a ceremony in which the Scots are purged and exalted by the shedding of sacred blood in the King's cause, even as mankind was once purged by the shedding of Christ's sacred blood on Golgotha. Only men in battle, who bathe in their own and their enemies' blood, are able to partake, bodily and symbolically, in the divinity of the state. As Christ's blood streaming in the firmament offers everlasting life to the worshipper, so the sacred blood of battle yields immortality to Macbeth and Banquo as Bellona's deathless bridegrooms and as participants in the greater life of the state (Macbeth will be king, Banquo will beget kings). By the same token, those who repudiate the god-king must be sacrificed, their treasonous heresies confessed in public, like Cawdor's, their heads exhibited on the battlements, like McDonwald's, to proclaim their mortality, the falseness of their gods and, by implication, the holiness of the victors. Much the same thing went on throughout Shakespeare's life when "treasonous" Catholic priests like Edmund Campion were sent to Tyburn to be hanged, cut down alive, and not only unseamed like McDonwald but disembowelled and dismembered as well.

In René Girard's formula, the indiscriminate bloodshed of the battlefield would be concluded by a scapegoat sacrifice that would safely "ground" the current of violence. Here, however, the battle itself is both the disease of violence and its cure, the *pharmakon* that is ambiguously both poisonous and medicinal.[18] Or, in informational terms, it is both a source of noise and a matrix of meaning. On the battlefield, violence erodes cultural distinctions, even the fundamental distinction between "us" and "them"; yet its function is to reaffirm and recreate distinctions by singling out, not scapegoat victims, but heroic survivors. Thus cultural life is renewed in death.

ROYAL REPLETION

The meanings I have been attributing to Scottish violence are obviously not derived from the battle as such, which of course we do not see, but from the Captain's report of it to the King. Perhaps this helps explain Shakespeare's failure to stage the fighting. For if the battle is entropic, then in itself it is messageless noise, as essentially meaningless as the actual offstage noise that represents it. Meaning is founded on difference, but on the battlefield "differences" are contested so violently that distinctions, and therefore meanings, cease to exist. But the existence of Duncan, the royal difference that Shakespeare underscores by means of spatial-theatrical distance, creates meaning. Because of Duncan's absence from the fighting, the Captain separates himself from the warring mass and, thus discrete, interprets its actions for the King, giving noise a meaningful voice: "Hail, brave friend!" Malcolm cries, "Say to the King the knowledge of the broil / As thou didst leave it." From this standpoint the King gives significance to the battle, transforming its random motions into ritual action. As the source of cultural meaning, Duncan should possess a royal splendor, a primitive magnificence more pronounced than is usually the theatrical case. As king he symbolically feeds on violence and bloodshed. In his royal difference is the plenitude of meaning toward which lesser men rise first by killing for him—by distinguishing themselves from their dead foes—and then by receiving aggrandizing "additions," honors, gifts, and dignities bestowed by him.[19]

If Duncan is replete with meaning, a treasury of sacred cultural value, then his generosity is central to the ordering of Scots society. For what we see him doing after the battle is distributing cultural meaning in the form of honors and titles as well as actual wealth. As Marcel Mauss demonstrated in his famous study *The Gift*,[20] social order in archaic societies was maintained by the circulation of freely given goods, a form of unconstrained sharing that was modified later on by the advent of private property. In classical times the attenuated correlative of this giving fell under the head of "liberality." In his treatise *On Benefits,* Seneca ex-

plained the reciprocal action of liberality—giving, accepting, and
returning—in the figure of the *Three Graces,* in which form it was
conveyed to the Renaissance and given expression, for instance,
by Spenser in the *Shepheardes Calender.*[21] In Shakespeare it appears
explicitly in the first seventeen sonnets and in *Measure for Measure,*
where it takes a monetary turn with the idea that man must not
presume to own his talents or even his life, since these are merely
lent him by God and nature, to whom he must return both the
thanks due a benefactor and the interest due a creditor.[22]

In *Macbeth* these debts to God and nature are summed up in the
feudal bond between loyal subjects and their anointed king, the
embodiment of natural foison and divine grace. What his subjects
have is not their own but only held on account from him, as Lady
Macbeth acknowledges, albeit in a speech of heavy irony:

> Your servants ever
> Have theirs, themselves, and what is theirs, in compt
> To make their audit at your Highness' pleasure,
> Still to return your own.   (1.6.25)

Or as Macbeth himself says after the battle:

> The service and the loyalty I owe,
> In doing it, pays itself. Your Highness' part
> Is to receive our duties; and our duties
> Are to your throne and state children and servants,
> Which do but what they should, by doing everything
> Safe toward your love and honor.   (1.4.22)

Social order in Scotland is thus dependent not on free acts of giving, as in archaic societies, but on a form of feudal exchange in
which the King lends power, prestige, and wealth to his subjects,
who make their returns in loyal service, and in blood and life if
need be. This form of feudal exchange is in keeping with the
symbiosis of subject and ruler figured in Menenius's "tale of the
belly" in *Coriolanus* (1.1). Like Menenius's "belly," Duncan dis-
tributes the cultural food he receives to his subjects, the "bodily
parts." But the food he receives is not grain, as in Rome, but the
blood shed in his cause by his warrior subjects. Replete with this,
he then yields up portions of himself to them, like the pelican

reputed to suckle its offspring with its own blood and hence said in its selflessness to embody, along with the fox (cunning) and the lion (strength, courage), an essential attribute of ideal kingship.

Thus Duncan is a source of cultural life for his subjects. In fact in the technical term of Elizabethan times, he like God has the power to "create" men, as he creates Macbeth Thane of Cawdor and Malcolm Prince of Cumberland, or as King James himself created with the "baronetage" an entire new class of men in 1611. So Duncan culturally creates Macbeth, and having created him he sustains him: "we love him highly, / And shall continue our graces towards him" (1.6).

But this idyllic view of kings and subjects has a foreboding shadow, as the imagery of blood and self-sacrifice suggests. For from this perspective Duncan's death is implicit in his royal approval of Macbeth's battlefield murders. This is made clear when Duncan's "O valiant cousin, worthy gentleman!" is officially confirmed by his bestowing the Thaneship of Cawdor upon Macbeth. Although this is an act of gratitude that does Duncan credit as well as Macbeth, it is also a symbolic resurrection of a dead rebel and traitor. With a gracious gesture designed in part to terminate violence, Duncan confers distinction on it, and hence ironically licenses its undifferentiating powers. As a result the difference between Cawdor the treasonous rebel and thwarted king-killer and Macbeth the heroic loyalist and king-preserver is nominally dissolved. In Macbeth's ever-active imagination Duncan might as well have said, "Rise up Thane of Cawdor—and kill me!" For it is upon learning of this "addition" that Macbeth becomes truly ambitious for a crown: "Glamis, and Thane of Cawdor! / The greatest is behind." He is now caught up by the momentum of the Witches' fate, to which, so it must seem to him, even the King's actions unwittingly contribute.[23]

DIFFERENCES AND DISTINCTIONS

Let me sum up a bit. I have labored the opening scenes of the play in an effort to demonstrate that Macbeth's famous lines about life being a tale full of sound and fury, "signifying nothing" germinate in the violence depicted much earlier. In Scotland battlefield violence is simultaneously the end and the beginning of meaning. As the end of meaning it is a witches' cauldron into which men's bodies are cast—a cauldron in which cultural and individual distinctions, the hierarchical differences of Degree, even the difference between friend and foe dissolve in the universal stew of blood. Degree thus vizarded, as Ulysses says,

> Then every thing includes itself in power,
> Power into will, will into appetite,
> And appetite, an universal wolf,
> So doubly seconded with will and power,
> Must make perforce an universal'prey
> And last eat up himself.   (*Troilus*, 1.3)

But the battlefield is also the source of meaning, the place where the difference between life and death, victor and vanquished, and as Heraclitus says god and man is created. By producing survivors, the battle generates primal meanings, and on the basis of these the King constructs cultural meanings, conferring new distinctions of Degree with his "additions," honors, and "creations." It is appropriate that the King should do this since the battle itself has been a contest to determine whether the major cultural difference in Scotland, that between him and his subjects, is valid.

However, when Duncan makes Macbeth Thane of Cawdor he confers a distinction that makes no-difference. In fact it makes no-difference twice, for it elides not only the difference between Cawdor and Macbeth but also that between prophetic future and present fact. Echoing the Witches' "Hail to thee, Thane of Cawdor!" Duncan's "I create thee Thane of Cawdor" seals a bond in Macbeth's imagination between desire and destiny. And so it makes all the difference. It endows Macbeth not only with a sense of past achievement—"The greatest is behind," he says on hearing the news—but of future promise: the "greatest" may be behind, but "greatness" lies ahead, and greatness entails immortality.

"Immortality" may seem a somewhat greater word than I need to refer to Macbeth's desire for kingship, but as I have sought to show by focusing on the battle scenes, to transcend death by inflicting it on others and surviving is a sacred achievement within Scotland's religion of violence. To rise over the dead is virtually synonymous with rising in status in Scotland, and kingship constitutes the highest point above death, the point where the "most" is concentrated—most life, most power, most prestige, most meaning. Shakespeare reduces to its simplest form the fact that culture is a vast immortality project, a symbolic system by means of which man seeks to transcend his biological status and deny death.[24] In Macbeth's case the act that denies death and makes kingship possible is a kind of self-fathering violence.

FATHERING ONESELF

Violence and death have been Macbeth's matrices of meaning. It follows now that to maximize his meaning he must become a king and that to become a king he must kill a king. His murdering Duncan will be an "uncreating" act that inverts but also parallels Duncan's act of "creating" him Thane of Cawdor. "Inverts" because it is destructive and "de-meaning," an assault on both Duncan's life and his royal significance. "Parallels" because it too makes no-difference; it erases not only the difference between king and thane but all cultural differences as well. In the darkness of Duncan's bedchamber there are only two men, one to bleed and die and one to survive. That, at any rate, is how Macbeth wishes it were, a simple shift of violence from battlefield to bedchamber. But everything in him says it is not, says that Duncan is more than merely a body with blood in it. Indeed the murder is an attempt not on Duncan the man who can die so much as on that "more" which is his royal and even sacred meaning. And a large part of that meaning centers in fatherhood.

In the previous chapter I suggested that Macbeth's dark deed is a rather monstrous concoction, a murder that is also metaphorically a sexual act, and—as if that weren't bad enough—an incestuous sexual act to boot. This interpretation put a somewhat greater stress on the sexual implications of Macbeth's line "I have done the deed" than it did on the murder itself. But, to right the balance, if we have an act of Oedipal incest, we must also have an act of Oedipal parricide. From this standpoint we would stress the context of Macbeth's "I have done the deed," noting that it follows immediately upon Lady Macbeth's remark "Had he not resembled / My father as he slept, I had done it." This filling out of the Oedipal picture presents us with a Macbeth who incarnates the infantile desire to kill the father and possess the mother at the same time, thereby becoming, as Lady Macbeth would have Macbeth become, a "man." The child's wish for a violent and premature graduation into manhood corresponds to Macbeth's impatience to "feel now / The future in the instant."

This sort of Oedipal interpretation helps explain our feeling that beneath the surface of Macbeth's stated ambition lies a deep and irrational ambivalence that renders the act as abhorrent as it is compelling. The murder simply seems to mean more to Macbeth than one would expect of a professional unseamer of bodies. It is an act beyond expression, a deed without a name—as, to be sure, it was until Freud named it. Such a view helps us see why from the beginning Macbeth's mind is invaded not by thoughts of royal power and privilege but by "horrible imaginings," as though the murderous means were an end in itself, as though to kill a king were to be a king. In this light the symbolic value of the act is the perfection of Macbeth's self, his completion as a man. In killing Duncan, Macbeth denies his creaturely dependence and announces, in the phrase Freud used of the Oedipal complex, that he is father of himself: "All the instincts, the loving, the grateful, the sensual, the defiant, the self-assertive and independent—all are gratified in the wish to be the *father of himself*."[25]

Such an Oedipal view may seem reductive.[26] It may appear for instance to shrink the King into a father and the nation into a family, thus foreclosing on a much wider context of meaning. That wider context of meaning comes back into focus, however, if we expand the Oedipal concept by regarding Duncan as Scotland's cultural father, a common enough view in Shakespeare's time. As such, Duncan has, as I said, "created" Macbeth and continues to sustain him. Yet his very generosity, for all its graciousness, has defined Macbeth, for all his prowess, as inferior and dependent, the social equivalent of a child. And thus the murder may seem the expression of a childish desire for instant gratification, for a self-fulfillment so total as to be tantamount to a wish to have fathered oneself. If you are not a child but already a man, the only way to father yourself, to acquire total independence, is to be "so much more the man"—to be king, and hence to kill the King. Thus Macbeth strikes at his cultural "creator," and through him, at his divine Creator. For of course regicide subsumes deicide as well as parricide. As we might expect in this tri-minded play, Macbeth's act is symbolically tripled, becoming an assault upon the Almighty Father, the royal father, and the genetic father.

To expand the Oedipal context of meaning to its furthest reach, we could stress the deicidal implications of the murder. Although I have not come across it, someone must surely have proposed man's primal Fall as a mythic analogue to the murder of Duncan by Lord and Lady Macbeth. The parallels of plot are obvious: a beneficent divine father, feminine temptations of the hero to aspire high, an act of disobedience that generates disorder in nature as well as guilt and vulnerability in fallen man. In *The City of God* (14.13), Augustine has a passage that invites comparison to *Macbeth:*

> Our first parents fell into open disobedience because already they were secretly corrupted; for the evil act had never been done had not an evil will preceded it. And what is the origin of our evil will but pride? For "pride is the beginning of sin." And what is pride but the craving for undue exaltation?

A "craving for undue exaltation" accurately describes Macbeth's ambition for greatness, abetted as it is by his wife. Of course the Macbeths murder the "father," whereas Adam and Eve merely disobey Him. Yet our first parents were inspired like Lucifer by an impulse to deify themselves, to "be as gods," the serpent suggested, by knowing what God knew. Instead, they learn only what Macbeth learns, that in quest of divine immortality they have eaten the fruit "Of that Forbidden Tree," as Milton says, "whose mortal taste / Brought Death into the World, and all our woe." The wages of sin is death, and sin is a prideful craving for undue exaltation. Psychologically, of course, it is just the other way around: faced with the inexplicable fact of death man must invent a sinful cause, if not in his immediate self, then biblically in his ancestral self. To live with guilt is better than to die without meaning. The invention of the Fall is to death as Macbeth's invention of a "dagger of the mind" is to the murder of Duncan: it marshalls us the way that we were going.

If the Oedipal aspect of Macbeth's deed suggests at one end of the Great Chain of Being an impulse to divinity, it evokes at the other end an air of bestial evil. Appetite, becoming a universal wolf, violates the most fundamental tabus of culture. As usual in the tragedies, Shakespeare depicts culture as a thin veneer over savage man; "humane statute" only tenuously cages the beast within. Nevertheless, instead of merely pitting humane culture against natural savagery, Shakespeare blurs the boundaries of the two. Macbeth violates basic cultural tabus in murdering Duncan —performing a deed so inhuman that it has no name in the vocabulary of his society—and yet his deed issues, as I have been trying to show, from an impulse to transcend bestiality and achieve cultural distinction. Macbeth's evil takes its origin in his culture as much as it does in an untamed savage nature, in part because Scots culture is founded on savagery. He is not, after all, a Richard Crookback killing Henry VI as an iconoclastic assault on individual goodness and corporate royalty. Both men employ the same regicidal means to the same end, of establishing a maximum difference from other men and from the human condition. What this means, however, differs radically. For Richard, regicide is the act that proves him uniquely unnatural, a creature born with legs forward and teeth sharp. With "neither pity, love, nor fear," he can vaunt "I am myself alone!" as he stabs through Henry at a society that excludes him (*3 Henry VI,* 5.7).

Richard takes a Machiavellian delight in proclaiming his own psychopathic divorce from human nature and civilized society. But Macbeth, who has earned "golden opinions from all sorts of people," is by no means an outcast. He has no desire to hack at the fabric of society or topple a throne. Unlike Richard, who, having no immediate prospects of kingship himself, wants merely to eliminate Henry by murdering him, Macbeth wants less to destroy Duncan than to substitute for him, to become him. Thus Richard murders Henry VI contemptuously, indifferently, without "pity, love, nor fear," whereas Macbeth is horrified by what he does, a horror inspired by reverence. He does obeisance to

Duncan's royalty in the act of killing him. Richard embraces the bestial difference that sets him apart from and beneath human-kind. Macbeth unwillingly falls into bestiality in an effort to attain the regal difference that will raise him above beasts and other men. By virtue of his triune Oedipal project he will substitute himself for all of his fathers, thereby proclaiming with Richard "I am myself alone." But the apotheosis of self he hopes to find in kingship is lost in the achievement.

THE IMMORTALITY PROJECT

For Macbeth to substitute himself for all his "fathers" is to assert his independence from the past and to take total responsibility for the creation of his own life—to become godlike. Annotating Freud's notion of the Oedipal project as a symbolic fathering of oneself, Norman O. Brown says, "The essence of the Oedipal complex is the project of becoming God—in Spinoza's formula, *causa sui;* in Sartre's *être-en-soi-pour-soi.*"[27] This vaunting ambi-tion, however, subsides with the child's gradual realization that he is godlike only on parental sufferance, that in fearful fact he is a creature vulnerably at risk in an overwhelmingly dangerous world. Unable like other animals to survive by instinct alone, he must put his trust in adults during a sustained childhood that inev-itably leaves an imprint of helplessness in the psyche. The child's "fear of freedom"—his fear of being on his own without the equipment to survive—is repressed in the process of maturing, that is, of graduating from a dependence on parents to a depen-dence on a parental society.[28] "Security," Hecate says, "is mor-tals' chiefest enemy."

Macbeth follows this pattern only up to a point. He has his shel-tered place in society marked out for him—Thane of Glamis. Obedient to his culture, he defends his king in battle, risking his life but risking it in a sacred cause, and is rewarded by a higher place, Thane of Cawdor. He is now snugly lodged in the hierar-chy of Degree. Then comes the Witches' prophecy. Their words are not, as we might expect at such a juncture, the rumblings of repressed reality; they do not say, as the Soothsayer says to Cae-sar, "Beware the ides of March," with the implicit caution "You are not a god; you can die," but rather "You have escaped death; you will be a god." For although "king" in what they actually say —"All hail, Macbeth, that shalt be king hereafter!"—carries a nimbus of divinity in it, the "hereafter" does also; its dominant meaning is of course simple futurity, but it also suggests eternality, an eternality that immediately comes in question when they promise that Banquo will "get kings" though he be none. Even rhetorically at this point Macbeth's immortality is threatened by Banquo.

Nevertheless, the project of becoming God is sufficiently appealing for Macbeth to expose himself to the fear of freedom:

> that but this blow
> Might be the be-all and the end-all—here,
> But here, upon this bank and shoal of time,
> We'd jump the life to come.

What "life to come" is he willing to risk—the heavenly "hereafter" promised by God or the royal "hereafter" promised by the Witches? Or, obsessed as he is with immediate gratification, are all hereafters merely present possibilities for him? Whatever he means, it is clear that if the murderous "blow" could only prove finite and circumscribed, then kingship and present greatness would substitute in his mind for God and everlasting glory.

However, the self-fathering act that would propel Macbeth toward deathless divinity also exposes him to all the helpless insecurity of childhood. How could it be otherwise when he kills so many "fathers" at once? When he leaves Duncan's chambers it is certainly not as a god, and less as a man than as a child awakened from a terrifying nightmare in which he murders all that stands between himself and his own mortal vulnerability:

> Still it cried "Sleep no more!" to all the house;
> "Glamis hath murdered sleep, and therefore Cawdor
> Shall sleep no more; Macbeth shall sleep no more."

To murder sleep is to raze the wall of cultural repression that keeps the terrors of reality at bay and lets man rest secure within the body of his society. Like a host of tragic and quasi-tragic heroes from Lucifer and Prometheus to Faustus, Macbeth has sought to substitute self-exaltation for the securities of culture, and in doing so he exposes himself to the frightening freedom of his truly vulnerable condition. From now on his nights will be spent in the "restless ecstasy" of "terrible dreams" from which he awakes in the inescapable certainty that he will die.

IMMORTALITY AS INCOMPLETION

In the previous chapter I spoke at some length about the ways in which Macbeth's murderous act is interminably undone. By virtue of its consequences, especially the escape of Malcolm and Donalbain, it has a kind of diabolic immortality, refusing to be, as Aristotle prescribed, whole and complete and of a certain magnitude. And since it is by means of this act that Macbeth seeks to perfect himself, Macbeth's own self cannot be whole, complete, "perfect." The self he seeks is identical with kingship, a state beyond manhood. But just as the regicidal deed remains incomplete, so Macbeth's kingship remains incomplete. He is in the position of the child striving for manhood but unable to find a definitive marker that guarantees its presence. Not even the throne and scepter can assure him that he is truly king, as Banquo's words suggest:

> Thou hast it now—King, Cawdor, Glamis, all,
> As the weird women promised, and I fear
> Thou play'dst most foully for it. Yet it was said
> It should not stand in thy posterity,
> But that myself should be the root and father
> Of many kings . . .   (3.1.1)

The plenitude Macbeth sought in pursuing the imperial theme is exhausted in the attainment. Far from vaulting him beyond death and human insecurity, Macbeth's royal ambition merely o'erleaps itself and falls on the other. "To be thus," he later laments, "is nothing, / But to be safely thus" (3.1.47).

From this time on Macbeth is not so much actively seeking immortality as attempting to ward off death. If he were Tamburlaine, all earthly ramparts reached, he might consider an assault on heaven itself. But Macbeth wants to terminate action, not prolong it. To ward off death means in practical terms to trammel up the consequences of the murder as best he can. Thus in the following scene we learn that he has sufficiently recovered himself to return to the scene he dared not look upon and slaughter Duncan's guards. Insofar as this staves off his own "death"—that is, the revelation of his guilt—it is the outside physical equivalent to his spiritual self-blinding: "To know my deed, 'twere best not know myself."

In each of the subsequent murders Macbeth preserves the image of his own deathlessness by mortalizing others. First Banquo, because "in his royalty of nature / Reigns that which would be feared" (3.1.49), but also because Banquo has an immortal dimension to him; he has a child and was promised much.

> Upon my head they placed a fruitless crown,
> And put a barren scepter in my gripe,
> Thence to be wrenched with an unlineal hand,
> No son of mine succeeding.   (3.1.60)

Immortality is now implicit not in the crown but in the succession. With no sons to succeed him on the throne, Macbeth will die. And Banquo will live. For although Lady Macbeth can say that in Banquo and Fleance "nature's copy's not eterne" (3.2.41), Banquo will royally "eterne-ize" himself through his filial line. This thought fills Macbeth's mind with scorpions, since it means that through his "issue" Banquo will stand astride Macbeth's dead body.

To deny death you must deny the body and locate your true identity in a surviving soul. That is easy enough for angels, not having been issued bodies in the first place, but for man—for religious man anyhow—the separation of soul from body can be accomplished only by dying, and that is what he wants to avoid in the first place. Stuck with a body, and a soul inconveniently ensconced in the pineal gland, as Descartes ascertained, man must substitute symbol and meaning for soul, letting himself be gathered into the enduring artifice of cultural significance before he dies. That this immortality is cultural instead of personal is irrelevant; it is the present experience of transcendence that counts—"to feel now / The future in the instant."

By the same token, to acknowledge death is to acknowledge the body. When Macbeth says of Banquo and Fleance "They are assailable," he denies their immortality by corporealizing them. Yet that is precisely what Banquo refuses to submit to. "With twenty trenched gashes on his head," he nevertheless survives in the form both of Fleance, to whom he cries "fly, fly, fly! / Thou mayest revenge" (3.3.22),[29] and of the ghost who keeps his dinner engagement. The deed is thus twice undone, and it renders Macbeth in two senses incomplete. When he hears of Fleance's escape he murmurs "I had else been perfect, / Whole as the marble, founded as the rock, / As broad and general as the casing air"; and when he sees the disembodied Banquo he complains—

> The time has been
> That when the brains were out, the man would die,
> And there an end; but now they rise again
> With twenty mortal murders on the crowns,
> And push us from our stools.   (3.4.79)

Banquo—"in whose royalty of nature / Reigns that which would be feared"—now reigns most fearfully indeed, seated in the royal place and crowned with mortal murders. Macbeth is at once unkinged and unmanned.

Macbeth's terror is caused not only by Banquo's inexplicable survival of death but by his meaning, for he is a *memento mori* to Macbeth himself: "It will have blood, they say; blood will have blood" (3.4.123). With blood and death in prospect, and quite certain that his kingship is not hedged round with Divine Right, Macbeth wonders how he stands with the demonic powers. Returning to the fens he discovers among other things that he is immune to death from a man of woman born. Yet at the same time he learns that from Banquo a line of kings stretches toward eternity. Thus the Witches offer him an apparent deathlessness but at the cost of his imperial immortality.

The murder of Macduff's family is, as I suggested in the previous chapter, a displaced version of the murder of Banquo. Macbeth finally kills a son, but not the right son, not Duncan's or Banquo's. And for once he fails to kill a father, the father who will kill him. In killing Macduff's "wife, his babes, and all unfortunate souls / That trace him in his line," Macbeth kills off Macduff's immortal part, his distinctively human meaning, all that would memorialize his existence. Without a "line" he is as it were but a single point, a finite, isolated being. Yet Macduff is immortal in another sense, having survived death by virtue of an unnatural birth. And because he is immortal in this manner, he will strip away Macbeth's immortality and leave him a hacked and headless body.

But before blood can have blood, ritual lustrations are required.

RITUAL SACRIFICE: THE *Pharmakos*

Let me briefly glance backward to see where we have been. In the opening battle we saw that violence is at once an entropic force, an undoer of cultural differences, and a source of cultural meaning in Scotland, a sacrificial bloodletting that charges men's lives with value. Most of all it charges the King's life with value, inasmuch as victory reaffirms his sacred status. His treasury of "greatness" replenished, he can shake the superflux to his loyal subjects in the form of additions and creations that reconstitute the differences of an ordered society. But this very process is self-destructive. The creation of differences, by both the Witches and Duncan, paradoxically perpetuates the undifferentiations of violence, causing the traitorous Thane of Cawdor to live on in Macbeth; causing Lady Macbeth to blur the distinction between maternal child-nourisher and defeminized child-killer; causing both to confuse the differences between beast, man, and king; all leading to a deed of darkness that grotesquely fuses king-subject, host-guest, father-son, mother-wife, and Creator-creature in what is at once an incestuous regicide-deicide-parricide.

In pursuing Macbeth's immortality project I have somewhat minimized the ritual aspect of violence. Let me return to that theme now by observing that critics have long been aware that from a certain distance the action of *Macbeth* assumes the contours of a purgation ritual in which a Scotland polluted by violence and evil is cured by excising the tyrant Macbeth.[30] In this connection we would expect René Girard's theories about the ritualization of violence to be helpful. I had better begin, however, by officially registering my awareness that *Macbeth* is a tragedy, not a ritual. For instance whereas ritual sacrifice will not do its job of grounding violence unless the role of scapegoat is arbitrarily assigned, tragic sacrifice will not achieve its aesthetic catharsis unless the role of tragic hero is earned. Ritual scapegoats are singled out; tragic heroes volunteer, albeit unwittingly. That means that guilt and innocence are readily distinguished in ritual—in fact, to distinguish them is the purpose of ritual—whereas in tragedy they are a mingled yarn. Thus ritual is designed to exonerate the community, tragedy to implicate its audience. In *Macbeth,* as I argued earlier, Shakespeare so fashions it that we all—author, actors, characters, audience—participate in the murder of Duncan. We have yet to see, however, whether he so manages it that we also participate in the killing of Duncan's murderer.

If ritual is a means of sanctioning violence, then we should expect it to play a significant part in the murder of Duncan, and so it does. Not that the murder is culturally sanctioned, but that to perform it Macbeth must fashion a fiction in which he loses his individual personality and assumes a ritual role. Othello adopts the same psychological strategy when he runs through a confused series of roles—judge, prosecutor, father confessor, and executioner—in order to dignify his "cause" of murdering Desdemona. Macbeth is less easily self-deluded. He does not pretend that evil is good but takes it for what it is and finds a kind of exalted rightness in aligning himself with maleficent powers. To break open "the Lord's anointed temple" (2.3.68), he imagines a counter-religion of violence, a cult of darkness whose goddess is Hecate and whose executive agents are withered murder, the wolf, and ravishing Tarquin.[31] The regicidal act thus takes on the aspect of a murderous "black mass" in which Lady Macbeth plays acolyte arranging beforehand the poisoned chalices, and Macbeth himself takes the role of murdering priest advancing upon Duncan with Crosslike dagger upraised before him as the sleeping guards cry out "God bless us" and "Amen."[32] The black mass aspect of Duncan's murder is a radical extension of the sacralizing of violence on the battlefield, where Macbeth was supposed to bathe in reeking wounds and memorize another Golgotha. He now literalizes the symbolism of the Mass, which does memorize Golgotha, by killing the Christ-figure in fact.

Macbeth's subsequent murders lack even the suggestion of ritual; butchery is butchery. Girard's "sacrificial crisis"—the breakdown of all cultural distinctions as violence is unleashed on the community—is in full force, as the descriptions of Scotland by Macduff and Ross in Act 4, Scene 3 indicate (3–7, 165–72). We discover there that Scotland is as miasmic as Thebes at the opening of *Oedipus Tyrannus.* When Ross arrives to report on things at home, Macduff says to Malcolm "See who comes here," and Malcolm replies "My countryman, but yet I know him not"—which calls to mind the arrival of the Captain in Act 1: "What bloody man is that?" It is as though the tide of blood has overflowed the battlefield and set all of Scotland awash. If so, it is Duncan's blood, for the murdered King has been, in the British manner, nationalized, his dying body becoming Scotland's body as the whole country "bleeds, and each new day a gash / Is added to her wounds" (4.3.40). "Who would have thought the old man to have had so much blood in him?" Clearly, powerful medicines are required to heal these injuries. Even Macbeth calls for a diagnosis and purgation of his land's diseased body (5.3.51), though by then it is the infectious invasion of the English that torments him.

In such cases Girard joins Macbeth in prescribing purgation and hence, because purgation must be accomplished by indirections, a scapegoat, a *pharmakos*—namely Macbeth. Macbeth may seem ill qualified to play the *pharmakos,* a role that must be assigned arbitrarily to an innocent if violence is to be terminated. Still, Jacques Derrida has shown that *pharmakos* is etymologically grounded in the meanings of both medicine and poison,[33] so that the sacrificial victim may be seen as both the disease of violence his community suffers from and its cure, the gutter into which all guilt is poured and the chalice from which grace will issue. In the often maligned Act 4, Scene 3, Macbeth is cast in this paradoxical role. His own private stock of evil, which is considerable, is augmented here to the point where he becomes monstrous beyond anything we have seen or even suspected. He is labeled a "tyrant" (12, 32, 36, 45), "an angry god" (17), "black" (52), a "devil . . . damned in evils" (56), as well as "bloody, / Luxurious, avaricious, false, deceitful, / Sudden, malicious, smacking of every sin / That has a name" (57–60). From the standpoint of the audience the more vilified he is the more innocent he becomes.

But the scapegoating of Macbeth is more than mere name-calling. It also depends on the symbolic displacement of guilt. Thus in this scene Malcolm, as though to compete with Macbeth in evil, portrays himself as more monstrous still. Malcolm does to himself verbally what he accused Macduff of intending to do actually. For Macduff, he says, may well have come to England to betray him, "To offer up a weak, poor, innocent lamb / To appease an angry god" (16). To avoid being sacrificed in this manner, Malcolm rhetorically betrays himself, sacrificing his lamb-like innocence in favor of appearing as an even angrier would-be god than Macbeth.

Malcolm takes on Macbeth's evils at such rhetorical length and with such studied ostentation that we cannot help feeling a radical disproportion between form and function in this scene. Surely Shakespeare goes far beyond any tactical need for Malcolm to test Macduff's loyalty. However, if we take a cue from Malcolm's remark about offering up "a weak, poor, innocent lamb" and consider the scene as a phase in a sacrificial rite, then Girard's thesis about ritual substitution seems surprisingly relevant:

> All sacrificial rites are based on two substitutions. The first is provided by generative violence, which substitutes a single victim for all the members of the community. The second, the only strictly ritualistic substitution, is that of a victim for the surrogate victim. As we know, it is essential that the victim be drawn from outside the community [so that his death will not stimulate further violence]. The surrogate victim, by contrast, is a member of the community.[34]

The logical member of the community to serve as surrogate victim is the king himself; however, the king, being sacred, is too valuable to die, so a ritual substitute, the real victim, is chosen. At this point in *Macbeth,* Malcolm plays the role of surrogate victim.

As Duncan's son, he is in moral reality the true king, the "innocent lamb" who for the moment ritually assumes the evils of the
actual scapegoat Macbeth and then purifies himself (and pollutes
Macbeth) by saying to Macduff—

> I put myself to thy direction, and
> Unspeak mine own detraction, here abjure
> The taints and blames I laid upon myself
> For strangers to my nature.   (4.1.122)

Macbeth, then, takes on the aspect of a ritual mock-king, the "real
victim" whose function is to absorb all rampant evils so that his
death will purge Scotland and restore the sacred King Duncan in
the form of his son Malcolm. But the killing of the mock king
must be exempt from the stigma of violence that has plagued the
country. His killers must be pure. Hence this ritual of self-pollu-
tion and purification whereby Malcolm becomes a worthy instrument of Scottish redemption. Because Macduff, who is to become the efficient cause of the mock-king's death, must also be
purified, his potential guilt as Macbeth's spy is washed away by
the blood of his murdered family. Malcolm's original suspicions
("He hath not touched you yet" [13]) evaporate with Ross's sorry
news.[35]

In effect both Malcolm and Macduff in this scene dip their
hands in the evil blood of Macbeth, then wash it away. The good
blood rhetorically shed here washes the bad blood of Macbeth
from their hands, in contrast of course to Lady Macbeth's futile
somnabulistic lustrations. Part of the purification of Malcolm and
Macduff here is a result of the sacralization of their cause through
the sanction of Edward the Confessor, whose healing touch cures
"evil" and whose backing inspires the expatriates to cry "Let's
make medicines of our great revenge" (214). By killing the *pharmakos* Macbeth, "revenge," itself part of the poisonous violence
that afflicts the diseased country, will become the purificatory
"medicines" that will heal her. The invasion of Scotland will not
be a continuation of violence but part of a ritual that will terminate
violence by purging the country of the *pharmakos*. Violence, we
are asked to believe, will at last end.

RITUAL DECONSTRUCTION

Act 4, Scene 3, then, appears to be synecdochic inasmuch as the
ritual assumption and purgation of evil by Malcolm and Macduff
mirrors in little the overall action of *Macbeth* itself, in which the
evils of battlefield violence generally directed at the King are concentrated in Macbeth, magnified to monstrous proportions, and
exorcised by a sacrificial ritual that enables Macduff to proclaim
"The time is free." Seen in this manner, Shakespeare's play is as
much a *pharmakos* as his hero. The violent impulses of Jacobean
England—with its religious and political paranoias in the after-
math of the Saint Bartholomew Massacre, the Essex Rebellion,
and the Gunpowder Plot—are apparently funneled into this play,
much as the evils of Scotland are funneled into Macbeth, and are
then purged by the violent action of ritualized drama. The diabo-
lization of Macbeth in Act 4—by reassociating him with the
Witches (4.1) and by making him a monster of evil (4.3)—allows
the audience the comforting illusion that evil can be reified and
expunged. Thus if Malcolm and Macduff are purified by dipping
their hands into the bad blood of Macbeth and then washing it off,
Shakespeare's audience is analogously purified by imaginatively
dipping their hands into the bad blood of his play and then washing it off by leaving the theater.

Knowing, however, how rarely Shakespeare exhibits positive
capability, we may have some doubt that things are so unequivocal. For one thing, this purgational formula does not take into account the Macbeth who is a tragic hero first and a ritual scapegoat
second, nor does it register some slightly disconcerting aspects of
the scene itself. Let me defer the issue of Macbeth as tragic hero
for the moment and consider the second problem.

What is disconcerting about the purificatory ritual in this scene
is that Shakespeare subtly undermines our assumption that Malcolm has fully washed the blood of Macbeth from his hands. The
first hint of this is Macduff's silence following Malcolm's sudden
erasure of his assumed evils. As Malcolm races on to tell how their
"warranted quarrel" can now proceed apace, he suddenly pauses
and says "Why are you silent?" (4.3.137). To which Macduff:

"Such welcome and unwelcome things at once / 'Tis hard to reconcile." Apparently his mind does not move as easily as Malcolm's between the poles of total guilt and total innocence, and for the moment the "weak, poor, innocent lamb" will not lie down in his imagination with "an angry god." Malcolm's deception may be as some have said, a pious fraud, like Edgar's deception of Gloucester at Dover, but the piety does not wholly eclipse the fraudulence.[36]

More troubling than this, however, is the attitude of Malcolm after Macduff receives the news about his murdered family. It is hard not to feel that Malcolm somewhat too hastily makes revolutionary grist of Macduff's grief:

> Be comforted.
> Let's make us medicines of our great revenge
> To cure this deadly grief.   (4.3.213)

Macduff replies: "He has no children. All my pretty ones?"

It is sometimes said that Macduff's "He has no children" refers to a childless Macbeth and hence expresses Macduff's disappointment that he cannot take his revenge in kind. But this renders the critic as insensitive to the situation as Malcolm himself. For it is precisely his pseudo-manliness—the too easy dismissal of a father's grief by a childless bystander—that gives force to Macduff's reply when Malcolm later says "Dispute it like a man" and Macduff says

> I shall do so;
> But I must also feel it as a man.
> I cannot but remember such things were,
> That were most precious to me. Did Heaven look on
> And would not take their part? Sinful Macduff,
> They were all struck for thee! Naught that I am,
> Not for their own demerits, but for mine,
> Fell slaughter on their souls.   (4.3.220)

In these exchanges Malcolm's notion of manliness, which calls for the transformation of humane feeling into violent resolve, troublingly resembles that which marshalled the Macbeths to the murder of his father.

It is not merely that Malcolm is deficient in feeling. He is deficient also in moral awareness, an affliction that attends the pursuit of high and holy causes, inasmuch as they invite melodramatic divisions of the "either you are with us or you are against us" variety. Thus Malcolm's earlier assumption and purgation of Macbeth-likeness in himself, which produced Macduff's troubled silence, comes into retroactive focus now through the lens of Macduff's response to grief. Instead of taking refuge in the role of innocent victim of outside evil, Macduff momentarily takes on tragic stature by accepting a percentage of responsibility for his terrible loss. For him, cast in the role of the Aristotelean good man with a flaw, guilt and innocence are not so readily distinguished as they are for Malcolm. In contrast to the latter's easy negation of evil in himself, Macduff's "not" is inextricably tied to his own "naught."[37]

Here then is a scene that is overtly committed to melodramatizing *Macbeth,* to dividing its moral world into the discrete hemispheres of good and evil, divine and demonic, medicinal purgers and diseased scapegoat. But Malcolm's ritual testing of Macduff, which is designed to maximize the differences between himself and Macbeth, employs a process of undifferentiation that momentarily creates an identity between the two, much as the violence of the battlefield yields meaningful distinctions only after a period of bloody likeness. As Macbeth became the King's approved defender by disengaging himself from McDonwald and Cawdor, his bloody and traitorous images, so Malcolm becomes the virtuous king-to-be by disengaging himself from a rhetorical merger with the tyrannical Macbeth. But Macbeth, as we know, did not completely purge himself of McDonwald and Cawdor, and the parallel may make us wonder if Malcolm has emerged unsullied from his verbal identification with Macbeth. By reactivating the concept of manliness at the end of the scene, Shakespeare makes an additional distinction between Malcolm and Macduff that impedes a partitioning of moral issues along either/or lines. When Macduff assumes the both/and-ness of a tragic character—

of one who is both good *and* evil, innocent *and* guilty—the purificatory action of the scene encounters the complexity of concrete
experience, which constitutionally resists the too easy absolutes
of ritual melodrama.

The effect of these counter-tendencies in the scene is slightly to
dislodge the audience's moral foothold in the "God's on our side"
conflict to come—not totally or even substantially to dislodge it,
but enough to make an unqualified identification with the invad-
ing forces less automatic.[38] Not of course that the war is unjusti-
fied. It is indeed a holy war, as all wars are. But when the rites
designed to sanctify it reach a point where its high priests are
vowing violent revenge and the king-to-be rejoices because "This
time goes manly," our militant righteousness should be tempered
by at least a faint sense of unease. "Manly," after all, is not a word
with which an audience of this play can feel entirely comfortable,
especially when it appears that Macduff's complex sense of its
meaning is yielding to Malcolm's simpler, disconcertingly
Macbeth-like version. Nevertheless, revenge is now Scotland's
medicine, violence her intent. With the "powers above" putting
on their instruments, it will not be long before bodies are unseamed and heads hoisted aloft.

THE TRAGIC VIEW

Malcolm can easily, Macduff with more difficulty, dissolve personal guilt in the ocean of Macbeth's evil and find in revenge a
medicine to cure both Scotland and themselves. But in the following scene we encounter Lady Macbeth's guilt, which will not
submit to ritual ablution and for which ultimately only the violence of self-revenge will serve as medicine. Thus we pass from
outward to inward violence, even as we pass from characters seen
exclusively from the outside, ritually, to one seen from the outside, by the Doctor and Gentlewoman, but in whom the inward
action of guilt is revealed in the failure of her own nocturnal ritual.

Actually the movement is from ritual to tragedy, a movement
that shapes the rhythm of Act 5 as Shakespeare's focus on guilt
and evil oscillates scene by scene between the inward perspective
of the Macbeths and the outward perspective of the high priests of

violent purgation. The result is a further refinement of the opposition of ritual and tragedy we began to see in the scene in England. We are reminded that ritual evil—the sort of evil Malcolm
claims in his mimesis of Macbeth in that scene—is an unmixed ab-
solute imposed from without. The scapegoat figure must become
a public sewer for all sins. To mitigate his evil, to adulterate it
with innocence or understanding, is to dilute his purgational potency. Thus it is fitting that the scapegoating of Macbeth leads to
Malcolm's final reference to "this dead butcher and his fiend-like
queen" (5.8.70).[39]

Tragic evil, on the other hand, originates within and imposes
itself outwardly on the world. The bad blood of murder flows
first in Macbeth's imagination, then in Duncan's bedchamber,
and finally throughout Scotland. The dagger in the mind marshalls the dagger in the hand into existence. Even the inward consequences of the murder project themselves outward. Macbeth's
self-estrangement—"To know my deed, 'twere best not know
myself"—ultimately pervades all of Scotland: "Alas, poor country, / Almost afraid to know itself" (4.3.164).

Yet ultimately Macbeth does know himself. Earlier I said we
could key an interpretation of *Macbeth* to the famous lines about
meaninglessness in the "Tomorrow" speech. Later I argued that
Macbeth's murder of Duncan is an extension of a kind of cultural
cannibalism first evident on the battlefield. Through killing,
Macbeth consumes the meanings of others, as he consumed the titles of Sinel and Cawdor. Now he will consume the sacred meaning of kingship by killing Duncan. But instead of "meaning," the
murder proves "de-meaning." Instead of a ritual sacrifice, it is a
gory killing in which Macbeth loses more meaning than he gains.
That is because he cannot fully suppress his moral awareness. Re-
versing the normal process of acculturation whereby unruly impulses are repressed and redirected, Macbeth "desublimates" or
profanes himself, employing a black-mass rite of murder to help
him repress cultural tabus and release battlefield impulses into the
bedchamber. This repression of "humane statute" requires a stern
hand and some practice, and Macbeth's first attempt, though it
gains him a crown, is psychologically disastrous. He renews his
efforts. Killing Banquo helps, but then Banquo returns, and he is

unmanned. Reinforced by a visit to the Witches, however, he kills Macduff's family and seems to have succeeded in his monstrous project. He has maximized his meaning, becoming immortal, if not in heavenly prospect, at least so far as men born of women are concerned.

Still, the very violence of Macbeth's efforts of repression testifies to a profound inner resistance. If the repellance of his deeds has made us forget this, putting us in the moral position of the Scots to whom he is merely a devil, Shakespeare reminds us of it by way of his wife. The unexpected surfacing of Lady Macbeth's guilt late in the play compels us to revise our earlier assessment of her. It now seems that her fiendishness—in her self-defeminizing speeches, for instance—was an armor of evil not only turned outward against the world but protecting and repressing a vulnerable conscience within. In Macbeth's case the voice of conscience speaks first, then is gradually subdued and eventually silenced by the clamor of evil. Yet, as with his wife earlier, evil is as much a means of repressing the good as it is an end in itself. The pace of violence must constantly be redoubled to outstrip "the pauser, reason."[40]

Yet near the end of the play reason catches up. Or, rather, Macbeth himself pauses and addresses himself to its disappearance. The world outside has grown increasingly meaningless. Events materialize randomly in tales told by unanticipated messengers. The arrival of ten thousand soldiers whitens the face of his servant, his wife's mind fails, the thanes fly, his wife dies, the wood begins to move. One thing after another does not make sense. The only meaning Macbeth clings to is the illusion of his invulnerability, his great difference from ordinary men:

> Till Birnam wood remove to Dunsinane,
> I cannot taint with fear. What's the boy Malcolm?
> Was he not born of woman? The spirits that know
> All mortal consequences have pronounced me thus:
> "Fear not, Macbeth; no man that's born of woman
> Shall e'er have power upon thee."   (5.3.2)

But Birnam wood removes to Dunsinane. A meaning beyond the apparent reach of language and sense dissolves into the ordinary when the soldiers carry their leafy camouflage toward the castle, just as another impossible meaning—Macbeth's immortality—will dissolve in the ordinariness of Macduff's Caesarean section.

This collapse of meanings seemingly beyond human ken reminds us that Macbeth's first murder was, like the Witches' conjurings, a deed without a name, at best an "it." To perform a deed that has no name in the language is to assume an identity that has no place in society. In seeking the fullest, most radically extreme meaning of self, a "manhood" somehow beyond manhood, a status above mortality, Macbeth becomes a nameless thing, a signified without a signifier. Thus in Act 4, Scene 3, we see Malcolm, Macduff, and Ross groping about in the vocabulary of vilification in search of names that will identify the tyrant. As a deity must be named before he can be worshipped and his powers evoked, so a devil must be conjured into a circle of names before he can be killed.

But it is Macbeth who names himself by naming his deed, by tracing its consequences, and his, to their ultimate end in the "Tomorrow" speech and the one beginning "I have lived long enough. My way of life / Is fallen into the sear, the yellow leaf." Although it is as easy at this point to sentimentalize Macbeth's *anagnorisis* as it is to condemn his criminality, he reveals none of Lear's sweeping compassion or profound moral insight here, no contrition, scarcely any feeling. He simply registers the consequences of his actions in the losses they entail: his wife's death, the death of love, honor, friendship, meaning itself. Yet implicit in the two famous speeches are guilt and the courage to acknowledge it, a stoic honesty that obliges the falling hero to recognize how the self he might have been has shriveled into what he now is. "When all that is within him," Menteith says, "does condemn / Itself for being there" (5.2.23), Macbeth is surely as loathe to reenter the sealed chambers of self as he once was to reenter those of Duncan. Yet at the hardest of times he has the courage to face not merely the circling enemies without but the far greater enemy within. The difficulty of the achievement is measured by the desperation of his need throughout the play to suppress self-knowledge.

Macbeth's *anagnorisis*—his willingness finally to acknowledge "all that is within" that condemns itself for being there—is a major reason why he transcends the melodramatic villain, the pathological case, and the ritual *pharmakos* to achieve tragic stature. This stature is enhanced by the fact that neither at this point nor further on, when the world closes even more menacingly around him, does he himself cast about for scapegoats, though in all justice he might have glanced ruefully in the direction of the Witches and certainly of his wife. Yet if his sense of personal failure implies a complexity of character that places him significantly above the simplicities of melodrama, it does not carry him so high that he yields his role as tragic hero for that of a morality play character. Without minimizing his crimes, he nevertheless keeps the fine line between tragic *anagnorisis* and Christian confession and penitence. The very enormity of his crimes, he seems to realize, sets him well beyond the shores of conventional mercy, so deeply plunged in evil that returning were more tedious than go o'er. At the very least he exhibits the stoic virtue of a man refusing the easy option of throwing in a losing hand. If his murder of Duncan in some respects represented an attempt at self-apotheosis, the child's desire (quickened by a spurious notion of manliness) for instant gratification of the wish to gain all and be all—god, father, world-consumer—Macbeth now, in registering his losses and self-degradings, earns title to a kind of manliness neither he nor his wife could once envisage.

VIOLENT ENDS / UNENDING VIOLENCE

The play ends as it began, with rebels seeking a king to kill. Or rather, seeking a butcher to kill. For part of the tragedy of the ending is that as we witness a divided Macbeth, a tyrant yet one who acknowledges repellence in himself as well as in the world outside him, his enemies close in to destroy in their view merely a "cursed usurper," a "butcher." Because in some measure Macbeth shares their judgment, he transcends their judgment. It is the destiny of tragic heroes to be isolated in self-division and nuance as the world they have violated returns to an oblivious but healing wholeness.

Macbeth's royal difference now is not marked off by dramatic distance as Duncan's was in the beginning. This king must descend into the tide of blood himself, and contribute to it. He goes into battle with one hope, merely to survive, and even that is insecurely held. Given the Witches' prophecy, the movement of Birnam Wood, like the dislodging of the golden bough, signals death:

> I 'gin to be weary of the sun,
> And wish the estate of the world were now undone.
> Ring the alarum-bell! Blow, wind! Come, wrack!
> At least we'll die with harness on our back.   (5.5.49)

Like Lear on the heath, Macbeth is being stripped of his illusions of greatness. "They told me I was everything," Lear says, " 'Tis a lie, I am not ague-proof." The Witches told Macbeth that he too was everything, and on the battlefield he was once "Bellona's bridegroom, lapped in proof." But now his mortal vulnerability is marked by his putting on and taking off his "proof" before battle; and though he wears "harness" in the field he is inwardly disarmed by the collapse of his protective prophecies. The news of Macduff's purifying unbirth cows his better part of man, yet even at this point, tied to the stake, he finds death preferable to public shame:

> I will not yield
> To kiss the ground before young Malcolm's feet
> And to be baited with the rabble's curse.   (5.8.28)

Though he claimed in the "Tomorrow" speech that death makes life meaningless, he still clings to the illusion of personal dignity, to a final meaningful difference between himself and other men. Since his killing career originated in the desire to assert that difference to the fullest, it is fitting now that he should prefer to be killed than to yield what remains of it.

But in the ensuing fight with Macduff, Macbeth loses his distinctive difference, as in the "Tomorrow" speech he lost his meaning. When the fighting begins, Macbeth, warrior that he is, must dominate Macduff. But when Macduff announces his unnatural birth, Macbeth's immortality drains away, and though he refuses to yield, the battle is no longer between Bellona's bridegroom and an ordinary man but between a witch-betrayed killer and a righteous revenger. This leveling action is repeated when according to the stage directions the two men *Exeunt, fighting. Alarums* and then *Enter fighting, and Macbeth slain.* Why should they exit and reenter; why should there not be simply one sustained battle, as in fact it is sometimes done?[41]

The likely answer is that the exit is designed to remind us of two prior instances of off-stage violence—the battle of Act 1 and the murder of Act 2. In each case the audience hears but cannot see the action—hears the trumpeted "Alarums" in the two battle scenes and, during the murder, the shriek of the owl, "the fatal bellman" (2.1.3). The undifferentiations of violence are thus aided by the pervasive darkness of the play (perhaps a dimming of the lights as Macbeth and Macduff commence fighting) and by the veil of unstaged action. So screened, Macbeth and Macduff now—like Macbeth and McDonwald, and Macbeth and Duncan earlier—are no long thanes and kings but simply creatures struggling to kill and survive. "Humane statute" stands in abeyance, the hierarchies of culture collapse, and for a few atavistic moments man returns to the chaos of primal violence.

But out of this entropy primal meanings also emerge, even as the two fighters emerge again on stage to stand distinguished— Macbeth raging viciously against the dying of the light, Macduff relentlessly driving him down. Then in a final shadowy action at the rear of the stage Macduff's sword descends on the neck of the fallen King, rendering his headless torso no different from any other. Then Macduff arises, lifts his visor, and displays the living head of a survivor beside the dead one of what Malcolm is soon to call a "butcher."

Though the play ends as it began, with heads mounted on high and bodies dismembered below, certain gestures have been made to suggest a resolution of violence. Lady Macbeth is done away with, by her own hand apparently, and Macbeth by Macduff's hand. No one survives Macbeth. On the field he is totally alone, without friends, thanes, soldiers, but most significantly without sons to whom he can cry like Banquo to Fleance "Fly, fly, / Thou mayest revenge!" Perhaps if revenge is at an end, then violence is at an end—which would seem to be the point of dramatizing the death of Siward's son. For although normally such a death would incite his father to revenge, here it produces merely a moment of soldierly satisfaction that the boy had his hurts "before," followed by a seemingly conclusive "His knell is knolled," at which point Macduff enters with the tyrant's head to proclaim "The time is free."

We have a ritualized ending then. Macbeth as the year-daimon in his wintry phase of death is slain, and the time is free because the *pharmakos* has carried off the pollutions of violent evil. But of course the year-daimon is also resurrected at once, taking its springtime form in Malcolm, who will begin planting newly with the time. But just as the battle returns us to the violence of the opening of the play, so Malcolm's proposed planting, his sowing of the seeds of honor, returns us to the moment of cultural "creation" with which Macbeth's search for meaning originated. Much as his father had done, Malcolm now announces:

> We shall not spend a large expense of time
> Before we reckon with your several loves,
> And make us even with you. My thanes and kinsmen,
> Henceforth be earls, the first that ever Scotland
> In such an honor named.   (5.8.60)

Perhaps we should take heart from the fact that with the creation of the rank of earl the thaneship of Cawdor ceases to exist. But it is hard not to feel uneasy with this new ordering of the Scots hierarchy when in the background, as if presiding over the action, stands the louring death's-head of Macbeth, in whose reeking wounds the victors are even now bathing.

The first gesture of the new king, then, is the last gesture of the play, to create the differences of Degree that proclaim an ordered society. However, as we now know, from just such differences contentious "differences" arise. In endless reciprocation violence is the birth and death of meaning, and order the womb and tomb of disorder. Hence when Malcolm ends the play by saying:

> So, thanks to all at once and to each one,
> Whom we invite to see us crowned at Scone

we cannot help thinking that the crowning of a king invites the killing of a king, and that Malcolm's invitation to everyone to meet again at Scone echoes something we heard before as the hurly-burly of battle was subsiding: "When shall we three meet again?" Between the new king's loyal defenders and Scone lie a good many wild and witch-ridden heaths.

Supplements

Undifferentiating Violence

As a historical supplement to the notion that violence undifferentiates, we might note that in the early seventeenth century the code of the duel forbade lower orders from challenging their "betters" because violence had been democritized by the popularization of the rapier and the pistol as weapons. Lawrence Stone comments with typical wit and learning:

> After about 1560 the broadsword began to give way to the needle-sharp rapier, with which it was only too easy to kill a man by running him through the body. The introduction of this new weapon thus had consequences exactly the reverse of that of the contraceptive: the one increases, the other decreases, the risks attendant upon two instinctive and pleasurable acts, fighting and making love.[1]

Further on:

> At first the code of the duel was socially beneficial in reducing faction fights and local blood-feuds, and in minimizing the consequences of the adoption of the rapier as the standard personal weapon of the gentleman. It also had an indirect, indeed largely accidental, consequence of blurring the distinction between gentry and nobility. Before the acceptance of the duel, an Elizabethan nobleman with his gang of liveried retainers at his heels could be as offensively contemptuous of the rights and dignity of his fellow citizens as a gangster in the streets and speakeasies of Chicago in the 1920's. . . . Now, however, the code put gentleman and nobleman on terms of equality. (P. 245)

Thus we see the process whereby social differences generate contentious differences that in turn undifferentiate the social classes. First, social differences are intact and defined in part by the fact that violence is at this time the special prerogative of the noble. With the introduction of the rapier and the pistol, however, whose ease of handling gives every man his share of violence, class differences are dissolved. Even the institution of the code of the duel accidentally contributes to this social undifferentiation brought on by the availability of violence to all. Then, finally, as Stone later points out, James I makes strenuous efforts between 1610 and 1618 to curb duelling and reinstate the social differences it helped undo.

Even considered in itself, the duel was an undifferentiating form of differentiation. That is, the code of honor governing the duel distinguished the precise gradations of insult and the kinds of response called for, beginning with a passing rudeness and leading up to the unpardonable giving of the lie. This chain of contentious being is parodied by Touchstone's inventory of replies to an expressed dislike of the cut of one's beard: the Retort Courteous, the Quip Modest, the Reply Churlish, the Reproof Valiant, the Countercheck Quarrelsome, "and so to the Lie Circumstantial and the Lie Direct" (*AYLI*, 5.5). Unfortunately, in the heat of the moment the first insult usually kindled a wick of aggression that shot inescapably up the hierarchy and exploded into dueling. When an innocently offensive remark at the bottom of the ladder is equivalent in effect to the Lie Direct at the top, the hierarchy of differences collapses, and the duel unleashes the very violence it is designed to control.

Prophecy, Deferral, and Form

The Witches' prophecies constitute a signifier, Macbeth's response the signified, and for him, fresh from the battlefield where he has gorged on death, "king" signifies "murder." Hence his sudden raptness which Banquo comments on (1.3.57), the same raptness he exhibits later in the scene when he tells us he is imagining murder (1.3.130 ff.) and still again when he moves somnambulistically toward Duncan's chamber to convert raptness into murder. This helps explain why for him the murder itself is tantamount to kingship, and why when he feels his kingship slipping from him his only remedy is to murder again and again in an effort to secure it.

Refusing to acknowledge the deferral of presence to which prophecy testifies, Macbeth illustrates the logocentricity that renders signifiers and signs transparent in its greediness for concepts and things. His futile pursuit of prophetic fulfillment not "hereafter" but "now" demonstrates that words can never catch up to their meanings. Just as signifiers strive toward nonverbal signifieds that upon attainment turn out to be merely further signifiers, so Macbeth chases a chain of signification in which "king" means "murder" which means "death-transcendence" which means "self-fulfillment" which means "manhood" which, imperfect and incomplete, leads round to "murder" again. The ostensible referent of all this, kingship, can be obtained by ceremonies of investiture at Scone, but kingship itself consists merely of signs—crown, throne, sceptre—that do not convincingly *mean* kingship to Macbeth himself. Hence more murders, until "kingship" means "tyrant" to all Scots, even in the end to Macbeth as well, at which point meaning disappears and all signs signify "nothing."

This suggests that Macbeth's experience might be thought of as a kind of existential assertion within a deconstructive world. Macbeth attempts as a sovereign individual to perform an act that apparently defies the moral canons of his culture, an act that will "perfect" him as a man. Yet the seeming originality of his regicide is compromised by the fact that while it violates the Christian "thou shalt not" it accords with the religion of violence that lies at a deeper level of motivation in Scots affairs. In this sense Duncan's murder and Macbeth's motives issue, as I have argued, from the battlefield. It is fitting then that Macbeth meets the Witches not before but after the battle, when his imagination is predisposed toward bloody thoughts, thus suggesting that the prophecies do not so much inspire his act as kindle in him a preexisting spark of desire. The fact that his motives are grounded in his culture qualifies the appearance of existential freedom in Macbeth's act, and at the same time confuses the seemingly clear-cut opposition of radical individualism (Macbeth the evil exception, the moral outsider) and cultural norms.

Moreover, the existential concept of self-defining action is both confirmed and denied. On the one hand Macbeth *is* defined as evil by the evil deed, yet on the other hand his own project of self-definition, his attempt to achieve "greatness" in kingship, is repeatedly frustrated: "I had else been perfect, / Whole as the marble, founded as the rock." His concept of self as rock-founded and capable of perfection and wholeness implies an Aristotelean concept of action as whole, complete, and of a certain magnitude. But Shakespeare repeatedly undoes the Aristotelean notion of action and hence the traditional concept of the independent self. Action and the self are not only unoriginal, unfree, and derivative from the past, from culture, but incomplete as well—open at both ends, as it were. Yet Macbeth persists in his futile efforts to close both deed and self, to loop the endlessly linear into a circle (by means of further linear acts). At the end, in the *anagnorisis* speech "My way of life," he admirably lives by his lights, both acknowledging his personal responsibility for what he has sorrily become and implicitly claiming that he has been his own self-fashioner. In the "Tomorrow" speech, however, he appears to recognize that individuality, originality, the sovereignty of self, are chimeras he has foolishly followed. Instead he is bound up in a vast illusory progress toward death likened significantly to theater, in which players speak the lines and perform the deeds that are set down for them. Nevertheless, or perhaps consequently, he goes into battle both to defy this daunting view of life and to play out to the end his part in it.

All this while, however, the play itself has been honoring its formal promises as the Witches' prophecies and Shakespeare's dramatic foretellings work in unison to create a sense of destiny in Scotland and of plot-fulfillment in the Globe. Thus the gap between signs and meanings widens toward nothingness for Macbeth because the gap between the Witches' prophecies and their foretold meanings narrows toward certainty. As Macbeth's efforts to loop the endless line of action into the completion of a circle prove increasingly futile, Shakespeare's play wheels

toward the formal closure of its cyclical shape—a closure, however, with a certain porousness or transparency yielding a faintly
ominous prospect of futurity as the newly-titled nobles try to sort
out their order of departure from one king-killing toward its consequence, a future king-crowning.

With this friction between the undoneness of Macbeth's murderous acts (and hence of his self) and the done-ness implied by
the fulfillment of the prophecies and the closures of aesthetic
form, where, we may wonder, should priority lie, in the form
of the play or in the experience it depicts? Are Macbeth's undoings a deconstructive comment on the apparent closure of
Shakespeare's dramatic deed, or does the Shakespearean form reassuringly enclose Macbeth's randomness, albeit with an air of
artifice? Since my own answer to these questions is a profound "I
don't know," they would seem to merit such fashionable terms as
aporia or "undecidability," but we might remind ourselves that
Murray Krieger anticipated the problem years ago in pointing to
the friction between tragic form and "tragic vision" and in focusing on works in which the vision eluded the form (*The Tragic
Vision* [Chicago: University of Chicago Press, 1960]), not to
mention of course Nietzsche and the uneasy tragic alliance of
Apollo and Dionysus.

Aggressive Giving

In *Crowds and Power* Elias Canetti says that a study of the original
documents of any religion reveals an astonishing unanimity of
belief in the frightening power of the dead:

> The first thing that strikes one is the universal *fear* of the dead. They are
> discontented and full of envy for those they have left behind. . . .
> Since the dead envy the living all the objects of daily life which they
> themselves have had to leave behind, it was originally customary for
> the living to keep nothing, or as little as possible, of what had belonged
> to the dead. Everything was put in the grave, or burnt with them. The
> huts they had lived in were abandoned and never used again; or they

were buried in their houses with all their property, to prove that no-one wanted to keep any of it.[2]

Later on I will discuss this in connection with Banquo's ghostly return; however, for the present let me suggest that this propitiatory giving of property to the dead has a temporally inverted version in a kind of talismanic giving to the living whose property is not lost but, rather, not yet acquired. The dead have lost what is rightfully theirs, so it must be returned to them; but in *Macbeth* Duncan's warriors have not yet obtained what they may feel is rightfully theirs—a share of the King's treasury of sacred meaning—so they must be given it, not all at once but in installments. Hence after the battle Duncan engages in a form of propitiatory giving of honors and property not merely to reward loyalty but to mollify the envy of the unfulfilled and to ward off regicide—a kind of royal inoculation against the social disease of ambition or a throwing of scraps to the circling wolves.

To pursue the implications of the scrap-throwing analogy: could one say that Duncan is like all the other Scots in murderousness but that being old he must do his killing more symbolically than they? It may seem odd to think of him as a killer, but it is he, after all, who has ordered his subjects into battle, saying in effect "Go kill for me—and if that fails, then die for me!" If they kill for him, then he is so much the greater. If they die in the process, he is exalted by their willingness to shed their blood for him. In either case he survives. Thus in a sense one could say that in killing Duncan Macbeth kills a man who by sending him into battle has if not actually tried to kill him at least put his life in jeopardy.

But killing by proxy is a relatively direct kind of symbolic aggression. More subtle is Duncan's giving of honors to his heroes. On the one hand this is a giving of his sacredness, a generous sharing of himself, designed ostensibly to reward their loyalty but also, at a more savage level, to fend off their hungry ambition. If he gave them nothing, they might well turn on him, as they all secretly know. An interesting question, then, is this: to what extent does this secret knowledge enter into and at a subtextual level transform the act of giving into an act of aggression? That is, it could be argued that Duncan's giving is not only self-protective, a purely defensive maneuver concealed in the guise of generosity, but an attack on those he gives to, a preemptive strike as it were.

The primitive parallel of this idea is the potlatch of the Kwakiutls of the Pacific Northwest. Among them the giving of gifts was an act of aggression symbolically equated with eating one's enemy. Thus one Kwakiutl chief destroyed "coppers" (coins) before his enemies and then cried, "Hap-hap-hap! I've eaten you. You are all in my belly now."[3] Here the killing effect of giving is explicit. Scotland, however, is a bit less savage than this, yet the symbolic point of giving may be no different. Giving, that is, is a form of killing that takes the subtler form of creating a burden of guilt. The thaneship, honors, and other gifts Duncan bestows on the Macbeths are so excessive that even Lady Macbeth is moved to say that they cannot repay the debt but can only be his "hermits," praying for his welfare (1.6.20). This is the kind of giving that impoverishes the receiver by putting him in such debt that he is filled with guilt.

The psychological strategy of such giving is of course to bind the guilty subject all the more closely to the all-powerful monarch. But it may have just the opposite effect. Oppressed by Duncan's generosity and his own guilt, Macbeth may feel that killing his royal creditor is the only way to free himself of his burden of debt. This is not of course his entire motive, but it combines murkily with others—passion for evil, ambition, the "manly" impulse toward self-transcendence, immortality, and Oedipal self-fathering—to deepen and complicate the origins of Macbeth's deed.

Undue Exaltation

To give Macbeth's immortality-project a historical context, we might note that there is evidence aplenty for an association of violence, social status, and immortality in Shakespeare's own time. Observe for instance how piously the Elizabethans, especially the "generation of 1560," as Anthony Esler calls it, worshiped the gods of honor and power.[4] Men like Essex, Robert Sidney, and Thomas Howard were driven to feats of heroism by a passion for conflict that cannot be accounted for in terms of natural aggression, greed, or political ambition. In a fairly literal sense these Elizabethan swashbucklers sought immortality. As Thomas Fenton said, "life dissolveth . . . but in true honor and good renown are laid up our monuments of perpetuity and fame so long as we live, and after our death they lift us to immortality."[5]

That honor and public esteem conferred immortality was of course an ancient belief, going back at least to the Homeric heroes, but it took on a special religious fervor in Elizabethan times. The immortality of fame was a means not merely of perpetuating oneself after death but of exalting oneself while still alive. The intoxication of performing brilliantly on jousting field or battlefield for an applauding queen and courtly audience could obliterate the 3 A.M. awareness of impending death. Hence arose what Hobbes calls man's "passion for glory," which attends his "perpetuall and restlesse desire of Power after power, that ceaseth onely in Death,"[6] or what Arthur O. Lovejoy calls "approbativeness," a "desire for esteem, admiration, and applause of others" that is "the universal, distinctive, and dominant passion of man."[7]

This approbativeness was surely the distinctive and dominant passion of Shakespeare's generation, so much so that honor, fame, and good repute could stand as secular substitutes for one's eternal soul. Witness Cassio's lament upon falling into disgrace in *Othello:*

> Reputation, reputation, reputation! O, I have lost my reputation! I have lost the immortal part of myself, and what remains is bestial. My reputation, Iago, my reputation! (2.3.256)

Iago's reply—"As I am an honest man, I thought you had received some bodily hurt; there is more sense in that than in reputation"—underscores the pathological dimension of Cassio's elegy for lost honor. In that connection, Robert Burton has a section in his *Anatomy* in which he treats of "philautia"—self-love, pride, vainglory, love of praise, etc.—as a sort of madness, the symptoms of which range in his discussion from a foolish love of flattery to a persuasion of one's godlikeness.[8]

Somewhat similarly, the Elizabethan cult of ambition, in the insatiable egotism of its desire to impress, constituted a thinly disguised drive toward divinity. Thus as Esler says,

> When he aspired for political power, then, the ambitious courtier saw his goal as a rare and marvelous thing, and associated it with the providential or miraculous power of divinity, the revered authority of law, and even the occult influences of the stars. Personal power, however underhandedly achieved, however sordidly materialistic its rewards, still possessed an aura of spiritual potency, a faint affinity with the supernatural.[9]

All of this is not a very far cry from Augustine's view of the source of original sin in the quotation I cited earlier (*The City of God,* 14.13):

> Our first parents fell into open disobedience because already they were secretly corrupted; for the evil act had never been done had not an evil will preceded it. And what is the origin of our evil will but pride? For "pride is the beginning of sin." And what is pride but the craving for undue exaltation?

This is a fairly apt description of Macbeth's quest for "greatness." In Scots society the road to exaltation is paved with violence, as it was in Shakespeare's England. Even in intellectual fields the passion for honor and power fostered a quarrelsome emulativeness. As Hiram Haydn says,

> Indeed, all the proponents of individualistic ethics—whether of force in political ethics, of honor in courtly ethics, or of instinct or inclination in naturalistic ethics—do have a common denominator in a certain assertive violence. They are all children of the "Ireful Virtue" rather than of Reason; they all profess some kind of *virtù* rather than virtue.[10]

One could catalog at length the associations of ambition, violence, and immortality in Elizabethan-Jacobean times, but enough has been said already to suggest that in *Macbeth* Shakespeare has given a somewhat archaic turn to this counter-religion, and in doing so suggests that Macbeth's murder, although a gross violation of cultural tabus, nevertheless has its matrix in culture, issuing as it does from the impulse to violent self-aggrandizement not merely permitted by Shakespeare's and Macbeth's societies but encouraged and rewarded.

Dogs and Degree

What is the point of the catalog of dogs in the scene in which Macbeth conscripts the two murderers (3.1.91 ff.)? The murderers declare themselves qualified for their bloody job by claiming "We are men, my liege." "Ay," Macbeth says, "in the catalogue ye go for men," as hounds, mongrels, spaniels, curs, shoughs, water-rugs, and demi-wolves "are clept / All by the name of dogs." But to its general doggy nature, he indicates, each kind has its "particular addition": its swiftness, subtlety, hunting ability, etc. "And so of men." And now, he says, "if you have a station in the file, / Not in the worst rank of manhood, say it"—and he will find employment for them. To which they reply that their lives are so miserable they will do anything.

The analogy is so labored as to suggest something significant. The major point of this, it seems, is to illustrate Macbeth's automatic assumption that the true man is to be defined as a killing creature. "Ay, in the catalogue ye go for men"; but catalogs are, as it were, horizontal listings, whereas Macbeth is interested in hierarchical listings. To qualify as an authentic man you must raise your head above the pack and kill, as he has himself risen above Glamis to be Cawdor and above Cawdor to be King of Scotland. Killing, self-aggrandizement, and social distinction are all deeply melded in his mind.

Moreover, the scene makes a distinction between those whose murder is an assault on the existing order and Macbeth whose murder is an affirmation of it. The refinements of Degree are meaningless to men whose lives are little removed from those of dogs. The murderers will not kill to acquire prestige or "greatness," but simply to survive, or, so alienated are they from Scotland's hierarchic society, they will kill merely, as one of them says, to "spite the world." Put money in their purse and they will rise—not socially but bodily—over the blood-boltered corpse of Banquo. For them the essential difference is not between the stations of Degree but simply between life and death. As a result Macbeth must find them somewhat incomprehensible and repellant, since he has no desire to spite the world but wants rather to endow himself more fully with its values. For him the great chain of societal being is not something to pull down but to climb up, by whatever means. In his skewed system of values, which is merely a radicalization of Scotland's own skewed system of values, Macbeth does obeisance to royalty in the very act of killing the King.

Returning Ghosts

Whether Banquo's Ghost is in Macbeth's chair or in his mind, as I shall suggest in the following note, its real or imagined presence testifies to a fear of the dead that is not peculiar to Macbeth. Above, in "Aggressive Giving," I quoted Elia Canetti's observations in *Crowds and Power* about the universal fear of the dead and the ways in which the living seek to mollify their spirits. For the sake of convenience, here is the quote again:

> The first thing that strikes one is the universal *fear* of the dead. They are discontented and full of envy for those they have left behind. . . . Since the dead envy the living all the objects of daily life which they themselves have had to leave behind, it was originally customary for the living to keep nothing, or as little as possible, of what had belonged to the dead. Everything was put in the grave, or burnt with them. The huts they had lived in were abandoned and never used again; or they were buried in their houses with all their property, to prove that no-one wanted to keep any of it.

If we apply Canetti's observations to the Ghost Scene we might argue that the Ghost returns, or in Macbeth's imagination wants to return, to recapture what it has lost. What it has apparently lost

is a throne and a crown. Of course Banquo lost these "posses-
sions" even before he was killed. That is, there is at least a suggestion that Banquo was himself tempted like Macbeth to hasten the
Witches' prophecy to its fulfillment and somehow seize the kingship for himself. On the fatal night, conveying a message to Macbeth, Banquo pauses and says to himself,

> A heavy summons lies like lead upon me,
> And yet I would not sleep. Merciful Powers,
> Restrain in me the cursed thoughts that nature
> Gives way to in repose!   (2.1.6)

This, coupled with his telling Macbeth "I dreamt last night of the
three weird sisters. To you they have showed some truth"
(2.1.21), could be taken as evidence that he too has had "horrible
imaginings." More likely, however, his remarks imply just the
opposite, that he has had troubling intuitions of Macbeth's dark
intent.

From Macbeth's perspective, though, Banquo may very well
have the same designs as he. Thus in any case—whether Banquo
makes his ghostly return seeking the throne and crown which he
thought (or which Macbeth thought he thought) his personal due
or which he thought the due of his heirs—the Ghost does, actually
or hallucinatorily, take Macbeth's royal seat of honor, and it is, as
Macbeth says, "crowned" with "twenty mortal murders"
(3.4.82). For a few moments, then, Banquo becomes King of
Scotland—or creates a prophetic image of kingship that forecasts
the reign of his descendant James I.

But the Ghost wants more than its lost property, as most spirits
of the dead do, according to Canetti. Even an extensive giving
back of property does not placate the dead, because their fundamental grievance is not the loss of goods but the loss of life:

> In the eyes of those who are still alive, everyone who is dead has suf-
> fered a defeat, which consists in *having been survived*. The dead cannot
> resign themselves to this injury which was inflicted on them, and so it
> is natural that they should want to inflict it on others.[11]

Or as Macbeth says, "It will have blood, they say; blood will have
blood" (3.4.123). More immediate than its demand for blood,

however, is its demand for what Macbeth has and it has not: manhood, life. The terrified Macbeth yields his manhood to the Ghost soon enough; he is, as Lady Macbeth says, "unmanned." And to regain his manhood he would even return life to the Ghost:

> What man dare, I dare.
> Approach thou like the rugged Russian bear,
> The armed rhinoceros, or the Hyrcan tiger;
> Take any shape but that, and my firm nerves
> Shall never tremble. *Or be alive again,*
> And dare me to the desert with thy sword;
> If trembling I inhabit then, protest me
> The baby of a girl. Hence, horrible shadow!
> Unreal mockery, hence!
>
> > [*Exit Ghost.*]
> > Why, so; being gone,
> I am a man again.   (3.4.100)

Moreover, the Ghost can be said to take not only Macbeth's manhood but his life, insofar as the Ghost is a *memento mori,* a prophetic Nemesis that portrays for him his own inevitable end, thus depriving him of his deathlessness and at the same time suggesting that Banquo, whose spirit survives his corporeal death, will also survive death in the line of future kings he has fathered.[12]

Banquo's Ghost / Our Ghost

Is Banquo's ghost "real" or only imagined by Macbeth? Although the answer seems to be supplied by the stage direction *"Enter the Ghost of Banquo, and sits in Macbeth's place"* (3.4.37) and by Simon Forman's testimony that a ghost did indeed enter during the 1611 performance he witnessed, perhaps one could make a case for a purely imagined Ghost. After all, Dr. Forman's seeing the Ghost on stage need not mean that it was materially, spiritually, or vaporously there; it means only that an actor was there. Both Oberon and Ariel appear on stage also, only to inform us that they are not there. We are supposed to unsee them. To some extent, perhaps, we are supposed to unsee Banquo's ghost as well. And if we are, what does that imply about our experience of Shakespeare's ghostly play?

In the first place, how do you prove the existence of a ghost? That is a question Bernardo and Marcellus ask about the Ghost in *Hamlet*. When they tell Horatio about it, he is skeptical: "Horatio says 'tis but our fantasy, / And will not let belief take hold of him" (1.1.23).. So of course they invite Horatio to see for himself, and when he does so they are afforded a small sarcastic revenge:

> How now, Horatio? You tremble and look pale.
> Is not this something more than fantasy?
>
> (1.1.53)

Seeing may be believing, but it does not guarantee that what one sees is actually there. More persuasive is seeing in company. Thus the Ghost in *Hamlet* is real because it is seen by Marcellus in company with Bernardo, and then by Horatio as well when he joins them, just as the Witches in *Macbeth* are real because they are seen by Banquo and Macbeth both.

But what if there are no corroborating witnesses? That is Brutus's plight in his tent outside Philippi when the stage direction says *"Enter the Ghost of Caesar"* and Brutus mutters doubtfully "Art thou anything?" (4.3.278). That the Ghost is anything, or something, cannot be ascertained until it answers Brutus, which it obligingly does with three ominous lines about meeting again at Philippi. No doubt about this Ghost. Both Brutus and the audience see it and hear it.

That is the case also with the dreaming Richard III in his tent the night before the battle of Bosworth Field. He has no witnesses as the ghosts of eight of his victims parade before him like the visions of Banquo's royal offspring when Macbeth revisits the Witches. At first we may regard these ghosts as the products of a suddenly activated conscience in the dreaming Richard. But that notion is quickly quelled by the fact that each ghost speaks aloud. In fact they end up chorusing cheek to jowl to the sleeping Richmond as well as to Richard. No doubt about these ghosts either.

By this measure we can authenticate a series of ghosts and spirits, including the prophesying spirit Asnath conjured up by the witch Margaret Jourdain in *2 Henry VI* (1.4), the ghosts of Post-humus's family in *Cymbeline* (5.4), and the spirits of Juno, Ceres, and Iris in the masque in *The Tempest* (4.1). All of these we not only see but hear. The one case in which spirits appear without speaking, and yet are clearly there, is in *1 Henry VI* when La Pu-celle conjures her fiends (5.3). The fiends do not speak, but that is because they cannot assent to her demands that they turn the tide of battle against the English. Their silence is itself an answer, as indicated by stage directions which say that "They walk, and speak not" and "They hang their heads" and "They shake their heads."

However, the character who is most like Macbeth at the ban-quet is Hamlet in Gertrude's chamber when his father's Ghost re-turns to whet his almost blunted purpose. Hamlet sees the Ghost, and we see the Ghost, but Gertrude says "all that is I see," and that does not include the spirit of her dead husband. If we were first-nighters at Shakespeare's play we might assume that although the Ghost is visibly in the Globe we are to imagine it as really only in the distracted globe of Hamlet's mind. And yet the Ghost speaks to Hamlet, and the audience hears it. That, and the fact that we are familiar with this Ghost from its appearances and speeches in Act 1, confirm its existence—and the moral blindness of Gertrude.

That gets us back to Banquo's Ghost, the lone exception to the rule. At the crowded banquet table Macbeth has witnesses aplenty to support him. "Prithee, see there!" he cries to his wife, "Behold! Look!" But though everyone looks, no one sees. Nor hears either. Macbeth challenges the Ghost to speak: "Why, what care I? If thou canst nod, speak too." But instead it leaves the stage, only to return again later. It would seem, then, that there is no Ghost in *Macbeth*. Not that there should be no Ghost on stage (although some stagings of the play have omitted the Ghost alto-gether) but that we are to regard the Ghost as a visible hallucina-tion. We are supposed to unsee it.

Why should Shakespeare want us to do this? To make the Ghost take a seat not in Macbeth's chair but in his imagination. To make it speak not aloud in the theater, a testimony to the existence of ghosts in Scotland, but silently in Macbeth's conscience, a testi-mony of the extent to which he is a victim not of the supernatural outside—either demonic forces or ghostly ones—but of the all too natural inside. Although Banquo's Ghost ultimately rises and takes its leave, enabling Macbeth to say "I am a man again," it is the ghost within that unmans him, a ghost that never fully makes an exit from his mind.

Still, even if we agreed that the Ghost is meant to be a fantasy, why should Shakespeare have it actually appear on stage in the form of an actor? Why not make it an invisible hallucination, like the "dagger of the mind" earlier? As I mentioned, some productions have done just this, and the actor who plays Macbeth has no difficulty conveying to the audience what he is experiencing. The trouble with this, however, is that it puts the audience on an equal footing with Lady Macbeth and the banqueting nobles. Let me explain.

I suggest that in the Ghost Scene Shakespeare is seeking by an inversion of technique that same effect he sought in the murder of Duncan. There, with the murder, he makes invisible what is real; now, with the Ghost, he makes visible what is unreal. As I argued earlier, the non-staging of the murder requires the audience to imagine its performance and hence to become Macbeth's accomplice in the act. Something of the same sort occurs now with the Ghost. For if it is an hallucination, then it is the product of Macbeth's guilty conscience, like the indelible blood on Lady Macbeth's hands in the sleepwalking scene. As such it can only be seen by those with the guilty knowledge of Banquo's murder, which of course eliminates the banqueting nobles and even Lady Macbeth, who is unaware that Banquo is dead. Macbeth is the only person at the banquet who knows about the murder.

Except of course for us the audience. For we, like the mysterious Third Murderer, showed up unexpectedly at the scene of Banquo's killing not merely to witness but imaginatively to help perpetrate the deed. Hence Shakespeare has us share Macbeth's sight of the Ghost as a reminder of our imaginative participation not merely in the invisible murder of Duncan but in all of Macbeth's dark deeds. Beyond this he reminds us of our complicity in the continuous dark deed that he himself is perpetrating, the play *Macbeth*.[13] He will not allow us to leave his theater under the smug assumption that we have been innocent onlookers of what has been done there, for we have been in on the doing. This entire ghostly play, he implies, does not lie outside our imaginations, dismissibly alien to our lives, any more than the Ghost lies outside Macbeth's.

And yet the play does lie partly outside our imaginations. We are not the sole creators of this dramatic deed, only collaborators. By the same token the Ghost is not entirely an hallucinatory product of Macbeth's imagination. After all, if the Ghost *is* seen by us, even if we are supposed to unsee it, then it has some sort of independent existence, perhaps in Scotland, certainly in the theater. When Lady Macbeth says, in echo of Gertrude to Hamlet—

> O proper stuff!
> This is the very painting of your fear.
> This is the air-drawn dagger which, you said,
> Led you to Duncan   (3.4.60)

—the ironic effect of her scorn is lost if we were, like her, seeing nothing.

This seems to undercut the rationalist argument against a real Ghost and in favor of a purely hallucinatory one. So it does. The problem is simply that the Ghost, like the play itself, evades the either/or categories of our logic. Shakespeare's own imagination in this play is preoccupied with the dissolution of the usual boundaries between mind and matter, imagination and reality, ghostly presence and ghostly absence. The imagination is not an alternative to reality but continuous with it; and yet a dagger in the mind is by no means the same as a dagger in the hand.

I suggest, then, that in the Shakespearean spirit of negative capability we are being asked to accept the Ghost as a paradox. It is and it is not there—a kind of "horrible imagining" whose presence/absence is in keeping with Macbeth's claim on the heath that "nothing is / But what is not" (1.3). As Macbeth must come to terms with his Ghost, deciding whether or not to honor its claims on him and within him, we shall have to come to terms with our own ghost, a play whose elusive presence within and outside our imaginations is reflected in the mysteriousness of the Ghost it contains and does not contain.

Notes

PREFACE

1. I have in mind such critics as Frederick Jameson, *Marxism and Form* (Princeton: Princeton University Press, 1971) and especially *The Political Unconscious* (Ithaca: Cornell University Press, 1981); Terry Eagleton, *Marxism and Literary Criticism* (Berkeley and Los Angeles: University of California Press, 1976) and *Literary Theory* (Minneapolis: University of Minnesota Press, 1983); Frank Lentricchia, *After the New Criticism* (Chicago: University of Chicago Press, 1980); Edward Said, *Orientalism* (New York: Pantheon, 1978) and *Criticism between Culture and System* (Cambridge: Harvard University Press, 1981). In Renaissance studies: Stephen Greenblatt, with his influential *Renaissance Self-Fashioning: From More to Shakespeare* (Chicago: University of Chicago Press, 1980) and the collection of essays he has recently edited, called *The Power of Forms in the English Renaissance* (Norman, Ok.: Pilgrim Books, 1982); Louis Montrose in such articles as " 'Eliza, Queene of shepheardes,' and the Pastoral of Power," *English Literary Renaissance*, 10 (1980), pp. 153–82; Richard McCoy, *Sir Philip Sidney: Rebellion in Arcadia* (New Brunswick: Rutgers University Press, 1979); and Jonathan Goldberg, *James I and the Politics of Literature* (Baltimore: Johns Hopkins University Press, 1983).

2. Even critics as objectively oriented as E. D. Hirsch, however, admit that "we know what literature is only vaguely. . . . To define is to mark off boundaries distinguishing what is literature from what is not, but our knowledge of literature has no such defining boundaries; there are many cases about which we are not sure—important cases, not just peripheral ones" ("What Isn't Literature," in *What Is Literature?* ed. Paul Hernadi [Bloomington: Indiana University Press, 1978], p. 26).

3. Of course there are significant differences among the critics of power. A major one lies between those who like Stephen Greenblatt (note 1 above) not only dissolve the familiar distinction between literary and non-literary texts but even that between texts and an extra-linguistic

world, all the world being a textual stage, and on the other hand Marxists like Frederick Jameson and Terry Eagleton (note 1 above) who decry the textual solipsism (of either the New Critics or the Deconstructionists) that would divide us from the realities of class struggle.

4. Of course political interpretations can be made of any play, simply because plays cannot help depicting the exercise of power in some form or another, just as metadramatic interpretations can be made because all plays employ language, action, and illusion. But it is also true that one can get more feminist mileage, say, from *The Taming of the Shrew* than from *Julius Caesar,* and more (non-feminist) political mileage from the history plays than from *The Two Gentlemen of Verona.*

5. The most prominent examples are Henry N. Paul's *The Royal Play of Macbeth* with its definitive subtitle "When, why, and how it was written by Shakespeare" (New York: Octagon Books, 1971) and Lilian Winstanley's *Macbeth, King Lear, & Contemporary History* (Cambridge: Cambridge University Press, 1922). See also, in opposition to Paul, Michael Hawkins, "History, Politics, and *Macbeth*" in *Focus on Macbeth,* ed. John Russell Brown (London: Routledge & Kegan Paul, 1982), pp. 155–88.

6. My goose-quill phrase here puts me in direct opposition to Marx and Engels, who in commenting on Eugène Sue in *The Holy Family* say that to separate the writer from the historically situated man is to "enthuse over the *miracle-working* power of the pen." I am conscious of the fact that writers, like anyone else, are social beings, most immediately so in their reliance upon language, and that the terms "author" and "creative" may misleadingly suggest an activity that takes place in a vacuum. But Shakespeare, while he may have been an ordinary social being of his time, was by no means an ordinary writer of his or any other time. Marxist phrases like the "production of texts" may be more appropriate than "creation" when applied to Harlequin novels, late "Agatha Christie" mysteries written by committee, or even Petrarchan sonnets turned out to order, but when used of Shakespeare or Donne or Joyce they become symptomatic of a nearly fatal inability to distinguish between the run-of-the-mill and the runners of the mill, between crude mass reproduction for a fashion-conscious market and profoundly individual articulation for all seasons.

7. In fact, as Gayle Green says in defense of Shakespeare: "In view of the prevailing Renaissance ideology about women and in view of the material conditions of women's lives, what is surprising is not that Shakespeare failed to create female characters acceptable to contemporary feminists, but that he created characters who are as convincing as they are" ("Feminist Criticism and Marilyn French: With Such Friends, Who Needs Enemies," *Shakespeare Quarterly,* 34, no. 4 [Winter 1983], p. 484). That is, Shakespeare's treatment of women is somewhat like his treatment of the lower classes, whom he clearly regards as lower in the main, yet to whom in particular cases he lends pathos, dignity, and grace. As

Northrop Frye says somewhere, Shakespeare is not so much undemocratic as pre-democratic.

I should add that Shakespeare's somewhat oversimplified characterization of some women in the plays is probably as much a consequence of his having to write for boy actors as it is of his own culture-bound attitudes toward women. In this connection see the first chapter of Lisa Jardine's *Still Harping on Daughters* (New York: Barnes and Noble, 1983).

8. This combination of Hobbes, Freud, and social Darwinism is especially prominent in Harold Bloom's talk (in *The Anxiety of Influence* [1975], *Poetry and Repression* [1976], etc.) about Oedipal rivalry, "strong" and "weak" poems and interpretations, and the Nietzschean will-to-power that impels snarling poets and critics alike to grab for their share of the literary carcass by whatever means available.

9. Even a deconstructive critic like J. Hillis Miller, who argues for the undecidability of texts, does not mean by "undecidability" that all meanings are on an equal footing and anything goes. In an "Interview" with Robert Moynihan in *Criticism,* 24 (Spring 1982), Miller says: "When I say a work is undecidable or open-ended, that does not mean that there is not a better or worse reading of the work. The best reading is the one that identifies most exactly the possible alternative meanings between which it is impossible to decide" (p. 110).

10. As for power and politics within the critical establishment itself, it is worth noting that the most radical claims about repressive conformity have come from academic people publishing in academic journals and university presses. This institutional receptivity to challenge is not, it seems to me, merely a form of tactical containment—a cynical willingness to put up with toothless assaults—but a genuine openness to argument and persuasion. In fact, iconoclasts so quickly become ikons themselves these days that they resemble nothing quite so much as persons indignantly beating on open doors.

On "the politics of interpretation" see the book of that title edited by W. J. T. Mitchell (Chicago: University of Chicago Press, 1982, 1983), and with respect to Shakespeare, *Political Shakespeare,* ed. Jonathan Dollimore and Alan Sinfield (Ithaca: Cornell University Press, 1985). See also Murray Krieger, "In the Wake of Morality: The Thematic Underside of Recent Theory," *New Literary History,* 15 (1983–84), pp. 119–36, and "Post-New-Critical Fashions in Theory," *Indian Journal of American Studies,* 14, no. 2 (1984), pp. 189–206.

1. *Macbeth:* COUNTER-*Hamlet*

1. For a fuller discussion of many of the following comments about *Hamlet,* see my *To Be and Not To Be: Negation and Metadrama in Hamlet* (New York: Columbia University Press, 1983).

2. For an insightful discussion of language in *Macbeth,* see Lawrence

Danson, *Tragic Alphabet: Shakespeare's Drama of Language* (New Haven: Yale University Press, 1974), pp. 122–41.

3. René Girard, *Violence and the Sacred,* trans. Patrick Gregory (1972; reprint ed., Baltimore: Johns Hopkins University Press, 1977).

4. It may be significant, then, that the most frequent term for action in *Hamlet* is "act," whereas in *Macbeth* it is "do." "Act" of course has histrionic overtones, and thus helps underscore the oft-noted theatricality of *Hamlet* as it re-enacts the source play it re-acts to. *Macbeth*'s "do-done-deed," on the other hand, refers not to acting, to doing a part, but to executing and concluding. Though theatrical enough in itself, *Macbeth* addresses itself to historical instead of histrionic accomplishments.

A comparison of the incidence of the key actional words in the two plays is interesting, although a mere word-count is misleading since *Hamlet* is almost twice as long as *Macbeth* (29,551 words versus 16,436; 1,115 speeches versus 647). That means for instance that although "do" appears eighteen times in *Hamlet* and only fourteen times in *Macbeth,* it occurs in only 1.6 percent of the speeches in the longer play as compared to 2.2 percent in the shorter one. Statistics levels all differences and emphases, of course, but "act" and "action" usually carry histrionic overtones in Shakespeare—they certainly do in these two plays—so that their greater frequency in *Hamlet* does, it seems to me, reinforce the obviously greater theatricality of that play. Anyhow, if only to create an air of hard science and deep calculation, here are some comparisons:

	Hamlet	*Macbeth*
do:	18	14
done:	4	22
deed:	11	18
act:	17	7
action:	11	2

5. For a perceptive discussion of the "art of preparation" in *Macbeth* see Wolfgang Clemen, *Shakespeare's Dramatic Art: Collected Essays* (London: Methuen and Co., 1972), especially pp. 76–86.

6. Marjorie Garber discusses "dream and conscience" in the two plays in *Dream in Shakespeare: From Metaphor to Metamorphosis* (New Haven: Yale University Press, 1974), especially pp. 88–117.

7. This is a classic example of Kenneth Burke's "scene-act ratio," whereby the real or imagined environment contains or even creates acts that reflect its character; see *A Grammar of Motives and a Rhetoric of Motives* (Cleveland: World Publishing Co., 1962), pp. 3–7. With reference to *Macbeth* at this moment, see Arnold Stein's excellent analysis of "Macbeth and Word-Magic," *Sewanee Review,* 59 (Spring 1951), pp. 271–84.

8. Derrida underscores this retentional aspect when he says "The instituted trace cannot be thought without thinking the retention of difference within a structure of reference" (*Of Grammatology,* trans. Gayatri Chakravorty Spivak [Baltimore: Johns Hopkins University Press, 1975],

p. 51). In his *Structuralism and Hermeneutics* (New York: Columbia University Press, 1980) T. K. Seung argues that Derrida's account of linguistic differences is essentially conservative by virtue of being retentional and referential (pp. 252–54), though perhaps he takes too little account of the futuristic element of "deferring" in Derrida's *"différance."*

9. I am talking here about the temporal "deference" involved in "deferral," but Murray Krieger, I should note, sees "deference" playing an unacknowledged role in Derrida's concept of the trace, since the trace, instead of asserting a positive identity of its own, modestly defers to those absent traces which constitute it (as their trace). However, Krieger adds, Derrida's own term *"différance"* belies its purported character as a trace by "behaving most *un*deferentially," by parading its "capacity to contain its divergent meanings" very much as poetic signs do (*Theory of Criticism* [Baltimore: Johns Hopkins University Press, 1976], p. 232).

2. DONE AND UNDONE

1. My remarks about action here are rather loosely phrased. If the action of *Oedipus Tyrannus* is "Oedipus's search for the murderer," then it begins and ends within the play as presented. But if the action is "the self-destructive efforts of Laius, Jocasta, and Oedipus to escape prophecies," then it does not. I think the action is Oedipus's search for the murderer, simply because that is what is dramatized on stage. Or, rather, what we actually see on stage (not to put too fine a phenomenological edge on it) is the plot (a series of connected actions by various characters), from which we infer the governing action (the search) and the story (the logical and chronological sequence of events beginning with the prophecy given Laius and Jocasta before the birth of Oedipus). I don't know if Aristotle would accept this account of matters. Stephen Booth, in a thoughtful chapter on *Macbeth*, argues that Aristotle repeatedly confuses the play itself with what it depicts (*King Lear, Macbeth, Indefinition, & Tragedy* [New Haven: Yale University Press, 1983], pp. 81–118). The special virtue of *Macbeth*, Booth feels, is that it affords its audiences the disconcerting experience of indefinition and limitlessness within a reassuringly defined and limited work of dramatic art, a view that does not seem incompatible with Aristotle's concept of theatrical catharsis. Thus Booth finds that characters, speeches, ideas, and, most importantly from my standpoint, actions will not stay within limits. He and I are both anticipated in this view of action by Terry Eagleton's excellent brief chapter in *Shakespeare and Society* (New York: Schocken Books, 1967)—e.g., "Every action done to attain security mars itself: every act has a built-in flaw, a consequence which escapes, like Fleance, from the control of the actor and returns to plague him" (p. 131).

2. Shakespeare plays off the linear historical movement of Macbeth's actions against a cyclical withdrawal-and-return movement associated

with the revolution of the seasons and of life and death in nature. For a learned discussion of linear and cyclical time see Mircea Eliade's *Cosmos and History: The Myth of the Eternal Return* (New York: Harper and Brothers, 1959).

3. For a study of the grammar of *Macbeth* see Francis Berry's "*Macbeth: Tense and Mood*" in his *The Poet's Grammar: Person, Time and Mood in Poetry* (London: Routledge and Kegan Paul, 1958). In reference to the namelessness of the deed see Paul Jorgensen, "A Deed Without a Name," *Pacific Coast Studies in Shakespeare,* ed. Waldo F. McNeir and Thelma N. Greenfield (Eugene: University of Oregon Books, 1966), pp. 190–98. For an excellent analysis of the ways in which Macbeth psychologically avoids responsibility for his actions, see Matthew Proser's *The Heroic Image in Five Shakespearean Tragedies* (Princeton: Princeton University Press, 1965), pp. 51–91.

4. Edward S. Casey argues forcefully for the autonomy of the imagination in his *Imagining: A Phenomenological Study* (Bloomington: Indiana University Press, 1976).

5. This is from Robert B. Heilman's brilliant study, *Tragedy and Melodrama* (Seattle: University of Washington Press, 1971), p. 67.

6. Eric Partridge, *Shakespeare's Bawdy* (New York: E. P. Dutton & Co., 1960), p. 33. I might add that Freud's claims for the interdependence of Eros and Thanatos suggest that acts of violence are implicitly acts of love and vice versa. From a Freudian standpoint Macbeth's murderous deed is appropriately nameless because it originates in his unconscious, in the territory of the repressed. By repeatedly calling the deed "it" Shakespeare literalizes Freud's "Id," attributing to the deed the same radical alterity (other than Ego) that Freud intended for the Id. As I suggest later, the complex symbolism of the murder is consonant with the psychoanalytic "return of the repressed."

7. About the undoing of the deed of murder by erotic metaphor: I should add that all metaphors are reciprocally undoing, since the conceptual integrity of vehicle as well as tenor is called in doubt. In the present case, the metaphorizing of murder as coition deconstructs coition no less than murder, leaving the audience with an unnameable monster. To which a critic might ask, If this is commonly the case, why is it so particular here as to deserve attention? The reason it merits such scrutiny is simply because of the prominence of "undoings" in *Macbeth* and because of the extraordinary prominence of the murder of Duncan. Moreover the erotic metaphor is endowed with special deconstructive force, as I suggest in the following section, by the way in which Shakespeare has dealt with the deed in the theater.

Critics who have dealt briefly with the sexual aspects of the murder of Duncan include Jan Kott, *Shakespeare Our Contemporary,* trans. Boleslaw Taborski (Garden City, N.Y.: Doubleday, 1964), pp. 79–80; Ian Robinson, "The Witches and Macbeth," *Critical Review*, 11 (1968), p. 104; D. F. Rauber, "Macbeth, Macbeth, Macbeth," *Criticism*, 2 (1969), p. 61; and Robin Grove, "Multiplying villainies of nature," in *Focus on Macbeth*, ed. John Russell Brown (London: Routledge and Kegan Paul, 1982), pp. 132–33. For more extended discussions of sexuality in the play, see Dennis Biggins, "Sexuality, Witchcraft, and Violence in *Macbeth*," *Shakespeare Studies*, 8 (1975), pp. 255–77; Ralph Berry, *Shakespearean Structures* (London: Macmillan Press, 1981); Coppélia Kahn, *Man's Estate: Masculine Identity in Shakespeare* (Berkeley and Los Angeles: University of California Press, 1981), pp. 172–92; and Yasuhiro Ogawa, " 'Fair is Foul, and Foul is Fair': The 'Ambiviolent' Fiction in *Macbeth*," *Language and Culture*, 2 (1982), pp. 17–53.

In this connection King-Kok Cheung makes a good point about Macbeth's remark "Bring forth men-children only!" in response to his wife's speech about dashing out her babe's brains ("Shakespeare and Kierkegaard: 'Dread' in *Macbeth*," *Shakespeare Quarterly*, 35, no. 4 [Winter 1984]): "It is curious that a speech designed by Lady Macbeth to provoke murder should give rise to thoughts of patrimony in Macbeth, unless he too has come to equate virility with heartless aggression—males with mails of armor, mettle with steely metal. He is ready to prove his virility by translating his procreative impulse into a destructive one, his fear of female domination into masculine aggression" (p. 438).

8. In a very thorough analysis of sexuality, witchcraft, and violence in *Macbeth*, Dennis Biggins perceptively sums up: "The exchanges between Macbeth and his wife that lead up to Duncan's murder, tensioned as they are by an eroticism that is sometimes submerged, sometimes overt, but continuously present, culminate in the decisive act of violence, which is envisaged as a kind of rape" ("Sexuality, Witchcraft, and Violence," p. 266).

9. Nietzsche, incidentally, also associates deeds with the procreative process when he has Zarathustra say "Oh, my friends, that yourself be in your deed as the mother is in her child—let that be *your* word concerning virtue!" As Paul Zweig comments, "Value must arise from the deed, as the child from the mother. Action must be at once a mothering and fathering, a terrain of androgynous, self-delighting values" (*The Adventurer* [New York: Basic Books, 1974], p. 213).

10. See Molly Mahood, *Shakespeare's Wordplay* (London: Methuen and Co., 1957), p. 135.

11. For information about the Gunpowder Plot see Henry N. Paul, *The Royal Play of Macbeth* (New York: Octagon Books, 1971), pp. 226–47. Also Lilian Winstanley, *Macbeth, King Lear, & Contemporary History* (Cambridge: Cambridge University Press, 1922), pp. 53–64.

12. See in this connection Robert B. Heilman's insightful article, "The Criminal as Tragic Hero," *Shakespeare Survey*, 19 (1966), pp. 12–24, and

E. A. J. Honigman's chapter "*Macbeth:* The Murderer as Victim" in his *Shakespeare, Seven Tragedies* (London: Macmillan Press, 1976), pp. 126–49.

13. Various critics have denied that Macbeth primarily seeks kingship. That, according to R. A. Foakes, is his wife's desire; Macbeth is motivated by something more like "the urge to fulfill himself [as a killer]" ("Images of death: ambition in *Macbeth,*" in Brown, *Focus on Macbeth,* p. 26. In the same volume Brian Morris argues that royal power is not what Macbeth seeks but "greatness" or "status" ("The kingdom, the power and the glory in *Macbeth,*" p. 42). Norman Rabkin observes that Macbeth's lack of interest in the crown contributes to the inexplicability of his motives (*Shakespeare and the Problem of Meaning* [Chicago: University of Chicago Press, 1981], pp. 101–10). I discuss his views further on in this chapter, and in the following chapter I take a line similar to that of Foakes and Morris.

14. Bernard Spivack, *Shakespeare and the Allegory of Evil* (New York: Columbia University Press, 1958), pp. 2–59.

15. Not that Satan plays a dramatic role, only a subtextual moral one. Iago is no more allegorical of the Devil than *Othello* is a morality play, although a fair number of critics, E. E. Stoll in the lead (*Shakespeare Studies* [New York, 1927]), have regarded Iago as literally infernal. The trouble with this, as Robert B. Heilman observes, is that it risks "using the myth of evil as a substitute for the analysis of the individual." Still, as he goes on to say, it would be foolish not to recognize Iago's diabolic dimension. The trick is in keeping the mythic, the psychological, and the theatrical in balance. See his classic study of *Othello, Magic in the Web* (Lexington: University of Kentucky Press, 1956), especially "Iago: Beyond the Grievances," pp. 25–44.

16. One meaning of "rapt" is "raped" (both, along with "ravish," "raptor," and "raven," deriving from the Latin "rapere," a forceful seizure or carrying away). From this point of view, Macbeth, his imagination raped into raptness by the prophecies, becomes a raptor and rapes Duncan of life and crown, like the "mousing owl" that hawks at and kills a falcon (2.4.12). "Rapt" has, we might say, an ethereal and an earthy dimension—a romantic-religious turning of the soul toward the beloved or God (a carrying away of the soul from the body) and a sexual assault (a carrying away of the body itself). Shakespeare combines the two as Macbeth's soul is rapt with images of a corporeal rape that will part Duncan's body from his soul.

17. Wayne Shumaker, *The Occult Sciences in the Renaissance* (Berkeley: University of California Press, 1972), p. 72. See also Geoffrey Bullough, *Narrative and Dramatic Sources of Shakespeare,* 8 vols. (London: Routledge and Kegan Paul; New York: Columbia University Press, 1957–75), vol. 7, pp. 457–59 for a discussion of diabolic influence on the fantasy in *Macbeth,* with appropriate quotes from Burton's *Anatomy.*

18. It might even be argued that Macbeth's inventory of reasons against the deed and especially his imaging of Duncan's virtues as trumpet-tongued angels and of pity striding the blast or horsed on the air are not dissuasions but persuasions. By magnifying Duncan's goodness Macbeth magnifies his own evil. The very forbiddenness of the deed lends it seductiveness. To think the unthinkable is not only frightening but intoxicating. In the following section I try to suggest why the deed is unthinkable to a degree not accounted for by the political tabus against regicide.

19. For this and the following citations from Rabkin, see pp. 105–8 of his *Shakespeare and the Problem of Meaning*.

20. Stephen Booth, *King Lear, Macbeth, Indefinition, & Tragedy*, p. 97.

21. For a sustained analysis of the "manly image" Macbeth takes for a model, see Matthew Proser, *The Heroic Image in Five Shakespearean Tragedies*, pp. 51–91. Coppélia Kahn effectively argues that Macbeth "follows a pattern of imbibing encouragement from female sources, then attacking male antagonists" as he seeks the manly state—*Man's Estate*, p. 174.

22. Jacques Derrida, *Of Grammatology*, trans. Gayatri Chakravorty Spivak (Baltimore: Johns Hopkins University Press, 1976), pp. 141–64. See also "The Supplement of Copula: Philosophy *before* Linguistics," in *Textual Strategies*, ed. Josue V. Harrari (Ithaca: Cornell University Press, 1979), pp. 82–120. I like to think that Shakespeare and Derrida are to the concept of "augment/supplement" as the playwright and Richard Burbage were to the wench in John Manningham's wonderful account, which might be given the Derridean title "The Supplement of Copulation: William the Conqueror *before* Richard the Third": "Upon a time when Burbidge played Richard III there was a citizen grew so fair in liking with him that, before she went from the play, she appointed him to come that night unto her by the name of Richard the Third. Shakespeare, overhearing their conclusion, went before, was entertained and at his game ere Burbidge came. Then, message being brought that Richard the Third was at the door, Shakespeare caused return to be made that William the Conqueror was before Richard the Third."

23. Two illuminating studies of these delaying tactics in *Hamlet* are Robert Hapgood, "*Hamlet* Nearly Absurd: The Dramaturgy of Delay," *Tulane Drama Review* (1965), pp. 132–45, and Michael Goldman, "Hamlet and Our Problems" in his *Shakespeare and the Energies of Drama* (Princeton: Princeton University Press, 1972), pp. 74–93.

24. Macbeth's desires and our expectations clearly part company, however, with the issuance of the second set of prophecies, which differ from the first set in being designed to blunt Macbeth's passion for the future by saying in effect "Expect nothing to alter the present." But as the Witches assure Macbeth that he is safe from all but the impossible, Shakespeare assures us that the impossible will take place.

25. Prophecy is merely the most explicit species of dramatic anticipation; see for instance Wolfgang Clemen, "Shakespeare's Art of Prepa-

ration," in his *Shakespeare's Dramatic Art* (London: Methuen and Co., 1972), pp. 1–95. For an exhaustive examination of the play as an evolving performance before a hypothetical first-night audience, see Marvin Rosenberg's monumental *The Masks of Macbeth* (Berkeley and Los Angeles: and London: University of California Press, 1978). For more abstract discussions of the dramatic mode as form in temporal suspense, see Charles Morgan, "The Nature of Dramatic Illusion," *Essays by Divers Hands,* ed. R. W. Macan (London, 1933), pp. 61–77, and Susanne Langer, "The Dramatic Illusion," in her *Feeling and Form* (New York: Charles Scribners, 1953), pp. 306–25. Time-conscious critics have frequently remarked the future orientation of *Macbeth*. See Francis Berry, "*Macbeth:* Tense and Mood," in his *The Poet's Grammar;* Frank Kermode, *The Sense of an Ending* (Oxford: Oxford University Press, 1966), pp. 84–89; Frederick Turner, *Shakespeare and the Nature of Time* (Oxford: Oxford University Press, 1971), pp. 128–45; Ricardo J. Quinones, *The Renaissance Discovery of Time* (Cambridge: Harvard University Press, 1972), pp. 351–60; Wylie Sypher, *The Ethic of Time* (New York: Seabury Press, 1976), pp. 90–108; and Yasuhiro Ogawa, " 'Fair is Foul, and Foul is Fair,' " pp. 17–53.

3. *Macbeth:* VIOLENCE AND MEANING

1. Harry Berger, Jr., also finds violence endemic to Scotland; see "The Early Scenes of *Macbeth:* Preface to a New Interpretation," *ELH,* 47 (1980), pp. 1–31. Although Berger is more persuaded than I that all the characters in the play, including Duncan and Banquo, are infected by the miasma of evil, nevertheless our views often coincide. One of the earliest attempts to give violence its due in *Macbeth* is Jan Kott's "*Macbeth* or Death-Infected" in his *Shakespeare Our Contemporary,* trans. Boleslaw Taborski (Garden City, N.Y.: Doubleday, 1964). See also Laurence Michel, *The Thing Contained: Theory of the Tragic* (Bloomington: Indiana University Press, 1970), pp. 42–60; Wilbur Sanders, *The Dramatist and the Received Idea* (Cambridge: Cambridge University Press, 1968), pp. 253–307 and "*Macbeth,* What's Done, Is Done" in his *Shakespeare's Magnanimity* (New York: Oxford University Press, 1978); Maynard Mack, Jr., in *Killing the King* (New Haven: Yale University Press, 1973); R. A. Foakes, "Images of death: ambition in *Macbeth*" in *Focus on Macbeth,* ed. John Russell Brown (London: Routledge and Kegan Paul, 1982), pp. 7–29; and Bert O. States, "The Horses of *Macbeth*," forthcoming in the *Kenyon Review*.

2. On the subject of violence I am indebted to a number of authors including Elias Canetti, *Crowds and Power* (London: Gollancz, 1962); Konrad Lorenz, *On Aggression* (New York: Harcourt Brace Jovanovich, 1963); Lawrence Stone's chapter on "Power" in *The Crisis of the Aristoc-*

racy, 1558–1641 (Oxford: Oxford University Press, 1965), pp. 199–270; George Boas, "Warfare in the Cosmos," *Diogenes,* 78 (April-June 1972), pp. 38–51; Erich Fromm, *The Anatomy of Human Destructiveness* (New York: Holt, Rinehart and Winston, 1973); Eli Sagan, *Cannibalism: Human Aggression and Cultural Form* (New York: Harper and Row, 1974); and René Girard, *Violence and the Sacred,* trans. Patrick Gregory (1972; reprint ed., Baltimore: Johns Hopkins University Press, 1977).

3. Lorenz, *On Aggression,* pp. 109–38. I should add, however, that Lorenz's views have been contested in the twenty or so years since he published them. The "killer instinct" in man—proposed not only by Lorenz but by Raymond Dart ("The Predatory Transition from Ape to Man," 1953) and especially Robert Ardrey (*African Genesis,* 1961)—has been shown to be exaggerated (see Erich Fromm, *The Anatomy of Human Destructiveness* [note 2 above] and Ashley Montagu, *The Nature of Human Aggression* [Oxford: Oxford University Press, 1976]), and ethologists have since pointed out that many other animals besides man kill their own kind, including gulls, langurs, lions, hippos, hyenas, macaques, elephants, and chimpanzees (see Richard Morris, *Evolution and Human Nature* [New York: Seaview/Putnam, 1983, p. 113]). On the whole anthropologists tend to argue against, and ethologists for, the innate aggressiveness of man. Thus in *The Biology of Peace and War* (New York: Viking, 1979), the German ethologist Irenaus Eibl-Eibesfeldt holds that man's brain is programmed with an innate disposition for waging war, whereas those in the human sciences contend that wars result from a learned identification with supra-individual causes—religion, tribe, nation, etc. Men go to war less like wolves, it seems, than like sheep; and in some primitive societies the cruelty of war is deliberately minimized by imposing rules and restraints, such as unfeathered arrows that are difficult to aim, spears with blunted tips, and ritualized "scoring" that substitutes for killing. Even the U.S. Defense Department prided itself for a time on having developed a "clean bomb," though we have leave to doubt that it was inspired by hygienic motives.

4. Konrad Lorenz, *King Solomon's Ring* (New York: Harper and Row, 1952), pp. 206 ff. Perhaps it is worth noting that Lorenz's claim that morality is man's version of the animal's instinctive inhibitions is based on the familiar assumption that culture is clearly discrete from nature, for which it substitutes, an assumption passionately held by those Rousseau-ists of the health food stores for whom "natural" is the most transcendental of all signifiers. But as Derrida has demonstrated, the relation between culture and nature is supplemental, not oppositional (see *Of Grammatology,* trans. Gayatri Chakravorty Spivak [Baltimore: Johns Hopkins University Press, 1976], esp. Part 2, "Nature, Culture, Writing"). In searching for the purely natural we keep encountering the cultural. In the present case, the wolf's instinctive brake on killing its own kind is itself a "cultural supplement" to its more primary natural impulse to kill.

5. Bernard Spivack, *Shakespeare and the Allegory of Evil* (New York: Columbia University Press, 1958), pp. 28–49. On this issue see also J. I. M. Stewart, *Character and Motive in Shakespeare* (London: Longmans, 1949), pp. 79–110.

6. René Girard, *Violence and the Sacred*. Girard's theory of violence is Heraclitean in that for him, as Robinson Jeffers puts it, "violence is the sire of all the world's values" ("The Bloody Sire"). Whereas Macbeth implies that primitive violence in Scotland has been purged by "humane statute," Girard holds that before humane statute the containment of violence was accomplished by communal ritual, and especially by scapegoat sacrifices. All societies are vulnerable to self-destructive violence not because man is instinctually aggressive but simply because the conditions of living generate mimetic rivalries brought about by shared desires—"I want that apple (woman, crown, etc.) because you want it." Mimetic rivalry causes an erosion of social and even individual differences. Wanting what you want, I become like you, and ultimately as competitive desire generates violence and effects a polarization of the community we all become viciously alike in pursuit of our violent ends. This epidemic spread of violence eventually reaches a point of "sacrificial crisis," a state of maximum cultural entropy that can be resolved only by transforming bad violence, which victimizes the warring community as a whole, into good violence—the sanctioned ritual sacrifice of a scapegoat—thereby reinstating the defining differences of an ordered society.

7. For an insightful survey of the symbolism of blood, see Carlo Levi, *Of Fear and Freedom,* trans. Adolphe Gourevitch (New York: Farrar, Straus, 1950), pp. 78–106. Harry Berger, Jr., "The Early Scenes of *Macbeth*," suggests the range of symbolic meaning of blood in *Macbeth* (p. 26).

8. Ernest Becker writes of how from an evolutionary standpoint man loses the protection of anonymity (within the herd, pack, tribe, etc.) as he is individuated by the uniqueness of his face. As a result "it is dangerous *to have a head*" (*Escape from Evil* [New York: Free Press, 1975], pp. 34–35). The psychological threats that attend such individuation occasion the title of Erich Fromm's book *Escape from Freedom* (New York: Rinehart, 1941).

9. Elias Canetti, *Crowds and Power,* p. 228. Jan Kott says "There is only one theme in *Macbeth:* murder. History has been reduced to its simplest form, to one image and one division: those who kill and those who are killed" (*Shakespeare Our Contemporary,* p. 77).

10. Otto Rank, *Will Therapy and Truth and Reality* (1936; reprint ed. in 1 vol., New York: Knopf, 1945), p. 130.

11. See Miguel de Unamuno's discussion of the "hunger for immortality" in *The Tragic Sense of Life in Men and Peoples,* trans. J. E. Crawford Flitch (1921; reprint ed., New York: Dover Publications, 1954), pp. 38–57. On man's efforts to transcend his fear of death by acquiring a sense of

immortality within culture, see in addition to Unamuno, Otto Rank, ibid., and *Beyond Psychology* (1941; reprint ed., New York: Dover Books, 1958); Norman O. Brown, *Life against Death* (New York: Random House, 1959); Alan Harrington, *The Immortalist* (New York: Random House, 1969); and especially Ernest Becker, *Denial of Death* (New York: Free Press, 1973) and *Escape from Evil*. See also Carlo Levi, *Of Fear and Freedom;* Jacques Choron, *Death and Western Thought* (New York: Macmillan, 1963); and Philip Aries, *Western Attitudes toward Death,* trans. Patricia M. Ranum (Baltimore: Johns Hopkins University Press, 1974).

12. E. S. C. Handy, *Polynesian Religion* (Honolulu, 1927), p. 31; also Eli Sagan, *Cannibalism,* pp. 1–21. To suggest the continuing relevance of such practices at their most primitive level, in *Escape from Evil,* p. 108, Ernest Becker cites an Associated Press dispatch from the "Cambodian Front Lines" which quotes a Sgt. Danh Hun on his treatment of his North Vietnamese enemies: "I try to cut them open while they're still dying or soon after they are dead. That way the livers give me the strength of my enemy. . . . [One day] when they attacked we got about 80 of them and everyone ate liver. (*Vancouver Sun,* British Columbia, Canada, Oct. 15, 1971)." See also in this connection the cannibalistic parallel of J. I. M. Stewart quoted in note 19 below.

13. Alice Griffin, ed., *The Sources of Ten Shakespearean Plays* (New York: Thomas Y. Crowell Company, 1966), pp. 245–46.

14. As Robert G. Hunter observes, "The indistinct figures of the merciless McDonwald, Sweno the Norway's king, and the Thane of Cawdor are important for the sense they give us that Macbeth's murder of Duncan is not, like Claudius' fratricide, a personal crime primarily, but rather one which a sizable proportion of the society is trying to commit and for which the entire society will inevitably suffer" (*Shakespeare and the Mystery of God's Judgments* [Athens: University of Georgia Press, 1976], p. 162).

15. Johan Huizinga, *Homo Ludens* (Boston: Beacon Press, 1955), p. 91.

16. Sir James Frazer, *The Golden Bough,* abridged ed. (New York: Macmillan, 1958), pp. 1–9, 812 ff.

17. Laurence Michel even hypothesizes that the Duncan of the play "*must,* on the circumstantial evidence of these first scenes, not only have usurped the throne himself, but have done it in a particularly foul and gory manner" (*The Thing Contained,* p. 56). My use of the King of the Wood myth supplements his half-playful hypothesis.

18. See Jacques Derrida, "The Pharmakon," in *Dissemination* (Chicago: University of Chicago Press, 1981), pp. 128–30.

19. At the same time, we can hardly help noting that Duncan is old and does not fight, that he is gracious and beneficent and "clear in his great office," as Macbeth says later, but also "meek." His Christian virtues will "plead like angels" against the "deep damnation of his taking-off," yet,

as Holinshed's McDonwald complained, Christian virtue is not Scots *virtù*. Duncan's sword has not smoked with bloody execution; he has not bathed in reeking wounds; and though he orders the execution of Cawdor after the battle, that is a remote and mediated form of violence—nothing like Macbeth's unseaming of McDonwald in the field. If the blood of violence is as sacred in its way as the blood of Christ, then the aged Duncan verges on losing contact with the sacred. From an orthodox religious standpoint, murdering Duncan is a sacrilege—an assault on God's vicar and hence on God Himself. From the standpoint of Scotland's religion of violence, however, regicide may be, like killing the King of the Wood, an inevitable purgative act, the slaying of a king whose cultural potency is waning. So viewed, Macbeth's crime is less in killing Duncan than in killing him prematurely out of a passion to have the future now. For as the battle has just confirmed, Duncan, though old, is still sacred and replete with meaning.

That Macbeth murders Duncan for deeply obscure, even primitive motives of the King of the Wood type—an absorption of divine or at least royal *mana*—is suggested by J. I. M. Stewart when he says: "The thought of murdering Duncan, first or new glimpsed in the recesses of his mind at the prompting of the witches, produces violent somatic disturbance, as the prospect of a ritual act of cannibalism may do in a Kwakiutl Indian. Nor is the parallel so outlandish as it may appear. For it is veritably the crime and not the crown that compels Macbeth, as it is the virtue that lies in the terrible and forbidden, and not the flavour of human flesh, that compels the savage" (*Character and Motive in Shakespeare*, pp. 93–94).

20. Marcell Mauss, *The Gift* (Glencoe: Free Press, 1958).

21. In a chapter in *Pagan Mysteries in the Renaissance*, revised ed. (New York: Norton, 1968), pp. 26–37, Edgar Wind explores classical interpretations of the Three Graces with special attention to Seneca's *On Benefits*.

22. The burden of the first seventeen sonnets is that the young man's beauty is not his to husband but has been lent to him by Nature, who expects repayment along the lines of the Duke's remarks to Antonio in *Measure for Measure*:

> Nature never lends
> The smallest scruple of her excellence
> But like a thrifty goddess she determines
> Herself the glory of a creditor,
> Both thanks and use.   (1.1)

In the young man's case, "use" should take the form of children. Related to the reciprocities of the Three Graces (note 21 above) is the Parable of the Talents (Matt. 25:14–30), and in an excellent article on Christian ritual in the *Macbeth*, Richard S. Ide notes that the remarks by Lady Macbeth that I quote in the following paragraph (from 1.6.27–30) are reminiscent of that parable and of the Offertory, in which "we offer back to the Sovereign ourselves and all He has given us" ("The Theatre of the Mind: An Essay on *Macbeth*," *ELH*, 42 [1975], p. 346).

23. Macbeth's kindled ambition is fanned into further life when Duncan makes Malcolm Prince of Cumberland. For Girard (*Violence and the Sacred*) this moment would combine with that when the Witches prophesied that Banquo would beget kings to represent the origin of mimetic desire, since Malcolm is now heir apparent and hence by definition desirous of the crown. Thus Macbeth:

> The Prince of Cumberland! That is a step
> On which I must fall down, or else o'erleap,
> For in my way it lies.   (1.4.47)

As the word "step" suggests, the concept of degree itself, the steps of social difference that rise like a staircase toward monarchy, shows Macbeth where his way lies. Duncan marshalls Macbeth the way that he was going. By lending out social rankings—Thane of Cawdor, Prince of Cumberland, etc.—Duncan engages in a form of royal sacrifice that fends off violence. He yields a portion of his plenitude to satisfy the craving for status that this system encourages. Yet this sacrificial act of sharing only whets the appetites of ambitious men like Macbeth. For the Elizabethan aspect of this, see "Undue Exaltation," section 6 in *Supplements*.

24. This argument, scattered throughout the works of Otto Rank, is gathered into a coherent presentation by Ernest Becker in *Denial of Death*, pp. 159–207. The symbolic gratification of moments of death-denying apotheosis is powerful indeed. If to be guilty—in disgrace with God— makes one vulnerable to death, then to be divinely favored makes one immortal. Then one "feels like a king," as Macbeth wants to do. Or like a queen—a beauty queen, for instance, or a Queen for a Day. Such secular beatifications usually reduce the recipient to tears of joy and disbelief, as though to say "Who would believe that I, who know too well my unworthiness, should be singled out to live forever, while these other mere 'finalists' are doomed to die?" Indeed, "finalist" suggests finitude of accomplishment as compared to the infinitude of "winner." In America, where the "winning is everything" ethic prevails, games are a life-or-death venture. If four hundred players enter the U.S. Open tennis tournament, for instance, only the survivor is a winner—the rest are "losers." Watching a losing NFL football team leave the field after a playoff game is like watching the Bataan death march. At the end of a losing season the coach is inevitably fired along with all his twelve assistant coaches—or as Macbeth would say "all unfortunate souls / That trace him in his line" (4.1.152). I might also mention a caption in the *Los Angeles Times* the day after the 1985 Super Bowl. In reference to the seemingly infallible young quarterback of the losing Miami Dolphins, it said "Marino Pressured into Revealing his Age and Mortality." The San Francisco Forty-Niners, it seems, brought the woods to Dunsinane.

25. Sigmund Freud, *Collected Papers,* ed. J. Riviere and J. Strachey (New York: International Psycho-Analytical Press, 1924–50), vol. 4, p. 201. Freud himself, as Paul Roazen notes, "came back again and again to the fantasy of being fatherless"—a fantasy, that is, reflecting his consciousness of having transcended his genetic background by becoming the father of psychoanalysis (*Freud: Political and Social Thought* [New York: Vintage Books, 1970], pp. 176–81). See also Ernest Becker, *Denial of Death,* pp. 105 ff., and Coppélia Kahn, whose interpretation of the play is founded on the notion that Macbeth is struggling toward a perverted manhood under the guidance of his wife-mother—"Milking Babe and Bloody Man" in her *Man's Estate: Masculine Identity in Shakespeare* (Berkeley: University of California Press, 1981), esp. pp. 172–92. Matthew Proser's excellent chapter on the play derives Macbeth's motives from the manliness required of the soldier-hero— *The Heroic Image in Five Shakespearean Tragedies* (Princeton: Princeton University Press, 1965).

26. In *Shakespeare and the Problem of Meaning* (Chicago: University of Chicago Press, 1981), pp. 106–10, Norman Rabkin discusses the virtues and drawbacks of a parricidal reading of the scene.

27. Norman O. Brown, *Life Against Death,* p. 118.

28. "Fear of Freedom" is the original title of Erich Fromm's *Escape from Freedom.*

29. One notes in passing the conjunction of immortality and violence in Banquo's dying words. Banquo's immortality is dependent on Fleance's escape, not merely because his genes will then survive but also because Fleance can revenge his death. For to be unrevenged—dismissed and forgotten—is to be truly dead ("Remember me!" the Ghost cries to Hamlet). Banquo's immortality is consequent on the immortality of violence. We are at that stage of social disintegration where violence is mimetically self-perpetuating, and man's only hope is to survive along with it however he can.

30. I believe the first critic to emphasize the myth and ritual aspects of *Macbeth* was Karl Simrock in *Die Quellen des Shakespeare* (Bonn: Marcus, 1872). But the most influential modern view of the play from that standpoint is in John Holloway's *The Story of the Night* (Lincoln: University of Nebraska Press, 1961), pp. 57–74. See also Norman Holland's chapter on the play in *The Shakespearean Imagination* (New York: Macmillan, 1964), pp. 50–71, esp. pp. 65–66.

31. As Richard S. Ide says, "Macbeth attempts to purge deep-seated misgivings about the murder by transmuting them into the solemnity of a black liturgy and attempts to free himself for the deed by identifying with the 'murdering creature' of the surrealistic world of night" ("The Theatre of the Mind," p. 348). See also Arnold Stein's insightful "Macbeth and Word-Magic," *Sewanee Review,* 59 (1951), pp. 271–84.

32. To judge from Macduff's remark in the following scene about con-

fusion having made his masterpiece (2.3.66) and from Macbeth's own claim that Duncan's "gashed stabs looked like a breach in nature / For ruin's wasteful entrance" (2.3.114), what was intended as a ceremonial sacrifice became transformed in its performance into a butchery, much as the ritual sacrifice of Caesar intended by Brutus did.

33. Derrida, *Dissemination*, pp. 128–30.

34. Girard, *Violence and the Sacred*, p. 269. Girard elsewhere discusses (pp. 101–18) how, rather like Malcolm in this scene, the sacred kings of Africa were ritually laden with guilt in order to resemble the scapegoat whose death would then purge king and community at once.

35. Macduff is also purified, and hence becomes a worthy purifier, by virtue of his not having been born of woman. As the first of many feminine sources of evil in Western culture, Eve, the betrayer of man and God, conveys original sin to us all; only baptism can rid us of her taint. Behind the myth is the old misogynous patriarchal notion that baptism purifies the infant who has suffered a contaminated passage through the body of a woman. Macduff is baptized in effect by Caesarian section. His freedom from feminine evil combines with Edward the Confessor's healing touch to sanctify the killing of Macbeth, who is deeply contaminated by contact with feminine figures like the Witches and his wife. For a stress on feminine influences in the play, see David B. Barron, "The Babe That Milks: An Organic Study of *Macbeth*," in *The Design Within: Psychoanalytic Approaches to Macbeth*, ed. Melvin D. Faber (New York: Science House, 1970); also Coppélia Kahn, "Milking Babe and Bloody Man" in her *Man's Estate*, pp. 172–92.

Insofar as the purgation of Scotland implies a corresponding catharsis of Shakespeare's English audience, this might have been done more easily. Giovanni della Casa noted in his *Il Galateo* (trans. Robert Peterson, 1576) that "Tragedies were devised at first that when they were plaid in the Theatres . . . they might draw forth teares out of their eyes that had neede to spend them [and] so they were by weeping healed of their infirmitie." This seems to him, however, a most roundabout method: "For if there be any that hath suche weeping disease, it will bee an easie matter to cure it with stronge Mustard or a smoaky house" (*Sixteenth Century English Prose*, ed. Karl J. Holzknecht [New York: Harper and Brothers, 1954], p. 307).

36. For a well-conducted argument in justification of Malcolm, see Camille Wells Slights' discussion in *The Casuistical Tradition in Shakespeare, Donne, Herbert, and Milton* (Princeton: Princeton University Press, 1981), pp. 124–26.

37. For a perceptive analysis of Macduff's notion of manhood and his mature awareness of his own share of guilt in Scotland, see Wilbur Sanders, *The Dramatist and the Received Idea*, pp. 272–74. As he concludes: "Only on this foundation of acknowledged personal guilt and responsibility can justice justly go into operation. And Macduff, as the one Scot

who has fully grasped this truth—Malcolm finds the tune merely 'manly' and is content with an 'enraged' heart—Macduff is the necessary agent of Macbeth's downfall" (274).

38. Speaking of the tendency of criticism to take mutually exclusive sides for or against Macbeth, Robert B. Heilman says "*Macbeth* . . . has a complexity of form which goes beyond that normally available to melodrama and morality play, where the issue prevents ambiguity of feeling and makes us clear-headed partisans." Nonetheless he feels that the play still falls short of the highest tragic achievement. See "The Criminal as Tragic Hero: Dramatic Methods," *Shakespeare Survey,* 19 (1966), p. 21. This is in contrast to the either/or position taken, for instance, by G. Wilson Knight when he speaks of the "opposition of life and death forces in *Macbeth,*" and regards "evil" as opposed to such concepts as "warrior-honour" and "imperial magnificence" (*The Imperial Theme* [London: Methuen and Co., 1958], pp. 125 ff.).

39. As Harry Berger, Jr., says ("Early Scenes of Shakespeare," p. 16): "Since we see more deeply than [the Scots] do into Macbeth, we are in a position to judge the extent to which they strip away the deprived humanity, the tormented consciousness and selfhood, he does have. Malcolm's final triumphant crowing over 'this dead butcher, and his fiend-like Queen' seems itself a mental and rhetorical act of butchery. . . ."

40. Francis Fergusson considers the "action" of the play best expressed by this phrase, to outrun "the pauser, reason"—see "*Macbeth* as the Imitation of an Action," *English Institute Essays 1951* (New York: Columbia University Press, 1952).

41. Marvin Rosenberg recounts the wonderfully various ways in which the fight between Macbeth and Macduff has been performed on stage—as indeed he exhaustively recounts throughout his book the various ways in which the entire play has been performed; see *The Masks of Macbeth* (Berkeley and Los Angeles: University of California Press, 1978), pp. 628–56.

SUPPLEMENTS

1. Lawrence Stone, *The Crisis of the Aristocracy, 1558–1641* (Oxford: Oxford University Press, 1965), p. 243.

2. Elias Canetti, *Crowds and Power* (London: Gollancz, 1962), p. 262.

3. Cited by Eli Sagan, *Cannibalism: Human Aggression and Cultural Form* (New York: Harper and Row, 1974), p. 112, from Clellan S. Ford in *Indians of the North Pacific Coast,* ed. Tom McFeat (Seattle: University of Washington Press, 1966), pp. 131–33.

4. Anthony Esler, *The aspiring mind of the Elizabethan younger generation* (Durham, N.C.: Duke University Press, 1966).

5. Thomas Fenton, *Golden Epistles* . . . (London, 1575), pp. 122v–123r; cited by Esler, ibid., p. 118.

6. Thomas Hobbes, *Leviathan,* ed. C. B. Macpherson (Baltimore: Penguin Books, 1968), p. 161.

7. Arthur O. Lovejoy, *Reflections on Human Nature* (Baltimore: Johns Hopkins University Press, 1961), pp. 128–30.

8. Robert Burton, *The Anatomy of Melancholy,* ed. Holbrook Jackson (New York: Vintage Books, 1977), pp. 292–300.

9. Esler, *Aspiring Mind,* p. 159; also Curtis B. Watson, *Shakespeare and the Renaissance Concept of Honor* (Princeton: Princeton University Press, 1960) and Hiram Haydn, *The Counter-Renaissance* (New York: Charles Scribner's Sons, 1950; Grove Press, 1960)—both of whom argue that the religion of honor provided vigorous competition to orthodox Christian humanism.

10. Haydn, *Counter-Renaissance,* p. 592.

11. Canetti, *Crowds and Power,* p. 263.

12. Matthew Proser has a good discussion of the Ghost as Nemesis in *The Heroic Image in Five Shakespearean Tragedies* (Princeton: Princeton University Press, 1965), pp. 76–79.

13. In " 'A New Gorgon': visual effects in *Macbeth*" (*Focus on Macbeth,* ed. John Russell Brown [London: Routledge & Kegan Paul, 1982]), D. J. Palmer notes that visual effects in *Macbeth* are not always visible, that "there are degrees of visibility, and the language of the play, with its powerful appeal to the visual imagination, mediates between the seen and the unseen" (p. 54). Many crucial events, persons, and objects in the play are unseen: the battles of Act 1, Lady Macbeth's infamous children, the air-borne dagger, the murder of Duncan, Lady Macbeth's conscience at this time, the murder of Lady Macduff, the estrangement of the Macbeths, Malcolm's self-assumed villainies, the English king, the damned spot, Lady Macbeth's presumed suicide, and possibly Macbeth's death. Thus to a more than usual degree the audience is required to imagine major actions and hence to collaborate in the creation of the play.

Index

Action: in *Hamlet* and *Macbeth*, 4–5; vs. acting, 16–19; and Aristotelean plot, 36; tragic, 39; and regressive progression, 40; and incompletion, 40–41; and identity, 41, 46; and transformation of Scotland, 41; in play as whole, 65–70

Anagnorisis: and Macbeth, 109–10; and "My way of life" speech, 118

Antigone, 34

Ardrey, Robert, 143 n.3

Aries, Philip, 145 n.11

Aristotle: and action, 33; and plot, 36; and nature of tragic hero, 51; and tragic hero, 105

Augmentation: as Derridean supplement, 57; and *Lucrece*, 57–58; and Sonnet 129, 58, 61; as ambitious desire, 62–65

Augustine: and original sin, 91; and pride, 123

Banquet scene and immortality, 97

Banquo's Ghost: and the envious dead, 125–27; presence or absence of, 127–31

Barron, David, 149 n.35

Becker, Ernest, 144 n.8, 145 nn.11, 12, 147 n.24, 148 n.25

Beginnings and unbeginnings, 34–35

Berger, Harry, Jr., 142 n.1, 144 n.7, 150 n.39

Berry, Francis, 138 n.3, 142 n.25

Berry, Ralph, 139 n.7

Biggins, Dennis, 139 nn.7, 8

Blood: and undifferentiating mortality, 77; as purifying, 83–84; and banquet scene, 97

Bloom, Harold, 135 n.8

Boas, George, 143 n.2

Booth, Stephen: and indefinition, 54; 137 n.1, 141 n.20

Brown, Norman O.: and self-divinization, 93; 145 n.11, 148 n.27

Buchanan, George, and *Rerum Scoticarum Historica,* 10

Bullough, Geoffrey, 140 n.17

Burke, Kenneth, 136 n.7

Burton, Robert: and self-love, 122–23; 151 n.8

Campion, Edmund, and sacrifice, 84

Canetti, Elias: and survival, 78; and power of the dead, 119; and fear of dead, 125–26; 142 n.2, 144 n.9, 150 n.2

Cannibalism, semantic, 74–75

Casey, Edward, 138 n.4

Cassio and lost reputation, 122

Cheung, King-Kok, 139 n.7

Children: and "increase," 63–65; as immortality projects, 97–98

Choron, Jacques, 145 n.11

Christ and battle scene, 83

Clemen, Wolfgang, 136 n.5, 141 n.25

"Consummation" and *Hamlet,* 13

Culture: and death, 79, 88–89; and savagery, 92–93

Danson, Lawrence, 135–36 n.2

Dart, Raymond, 143 n.3

Death: in *Hamlet* and *Macbeth,* 21; and